AKHIR 35

CANTIERI DI PISA

cantieri di pisa s.p.a. - via aurelia km. 334 - 56100 pisa - tel. (050) 500739 / 500740 - telex 590044 cantpii - telefax (050) 598026

La Vallée

M︳V Via Statale dei Giovi, 37 - Telefono 031/900359 - Fax 031/900971 - 22070 VERTEMATE (Como) Italy

CONTENTS

INTERNATIONAL MAGAZINE OF AUTOMOBILES AND OTHER OBJETS D'ART

N° 6 - MARCH 1994

Chief Editor
Roberto Merlo

*Contributors at
Ettore Bugatti Srl and
Bugatti Automobili S.p.a.*
Ivo Ceci
(Historical archive)
Giovanna Morena
(Cultural Centre)
Alessia Regazzoni
(Press Office Bugatti Automobili)
Karin Scanzoni
*(Press Office
EB Ettore Bugatti)*

Typesetting
Graphics department
Giorgio Nada Editore

Translations
Neil Davenport
(English)
Soget srl
(French)
Wolfang Schoene
(German)

Contributors to this issue
Renata Artioli
Romano Artioli
Giampaolo Benedini
Enrico Benzing
Gianni Cancellieri
Ivo Ceci
Gualtiero Coppe
Shotaro Kobayashi
Noriko Welponer
Giuseppe Maghenzani
Mario Merlo
Franco Zagari
Karin Scanzoni

Photographs
Bugatti Archives
Mantero Archives
Roberto Bigano
Arnaldo Castoldi
Elvio Deganello
Massimo Mantovani (Camera 22)
Roberto Merlo
Gigi Soldano
Roberto Sorrentino
Renzo Wieser
Franco Zagari

GIORGIO NADA EDITORE

*Head Office, administrative
and editorial office*
via Claudio Treves, 15/17
20090 Vimodrone (MI)- Italy
tel. 02/27301126 -
fax 02/27301454

Editorial coordination
Antonio Maffeis

EB Ettore Bugatti n° 6
ISBN 83-7911-115-9

Distributors
ITALY
Consorzio Distributori Associati
via Mario Alicata, 2f
40050 Monte San Pietro (BO)

FRANCE
Librairie du Collectionneur
4, Rue Cassette, 75006 Parigi
tel. 01/42.22.34.08 - fax 01/45.44.39.02

Trame/ Boulogne
62, Bld Jean Jaures, 92100 Boulogne
tel. 01/46.03.48.69 - fax 01/46.03.46.85

GREAT BRITAIN
Veloce Publishing Plc
Godmanstone - Dorset DT2 7AE
tel. 0300/341602 - fax 0300/341065

Menoshire Ltd
Unit 13, Wadsworth Business Centre
21 Wadworth Road, Perivale, Middlesex
tel. 081/5667343-4 - fax 081/9912439

GERMANY
Heel Verlag GmbH
Hauptstrasse 354
5330 Königswinter 1
tel. 02223/23027 - fax 02223/23028

HOLLAND
Cars & Books B.V.
G Oude Gracht 101
2011 GN-Haarlem
tel. 023/320595 - fax 023/327289

JAPAN
Hokuto Corporation
32-5 Minamidai 3-chome
Nakano-ku
Tokyo 164

UNITED STATES
Motorbooks International
729 Prospect Avenue
Osceola Wisconsin 54020

Howell Press
1147 River Road
Bay 2, Charlottesville, Virginia 22901
tel. 804-977-4006 - fax 804-971-7204

Mail order sales
Libreria dell'Automobile
corso Venezia, 43
20121 Milano
tel. 02/27301462-27301468
fax 02/27301454

Registration
at the Milan court
n. 188 21/3/1992

Color separations
Mediolanum Color Separation
Cologno Monzese (MI)

Printed by
Grafiche Editoriali Padane - Cremona

Advertising
TOP LEVEL s.a.s.
via Pasquale Paoli, 4 - Milan - Italy
tel. 02/89400021 - fax 58112701
© 1993 Giorgio Nada Editore, Vimodrone
(Milan)

Printed in Italy
*All rights reserved. No parts of this pubblication
may be reproduced, stored in a retrieval
system, or transmitted, in any form or by any
means, electronic, mechanical, photocopying,
recording or otherwise, without prior written
permission of Giorgio Nada Editore,
Vimodrone (Milan)*

Editorial	4
Bugatti and Lotus: Love and Marriage	6
Parallel Lives	10
Close Encounters of Technology and Style	16
The New Bugatti Architecture	20
Chassis and Suspension: Bugatti Innovation and Continuity	32
Past, Present and Future in the Realm of the Samurai	38
News	44
The Klausen's Second Coming	46
A True Gentleman Driver	52
Life and Movement in The Pastels of Ferreyra-Basso	56
New Blue Sensations	62
A Temple for the Bugatti Collections	66
A Global Conception of Beauty and Function	68
Mantero and the Bugatti Silk Road	74
Bugatti: A Marriage of Style and Culture	78

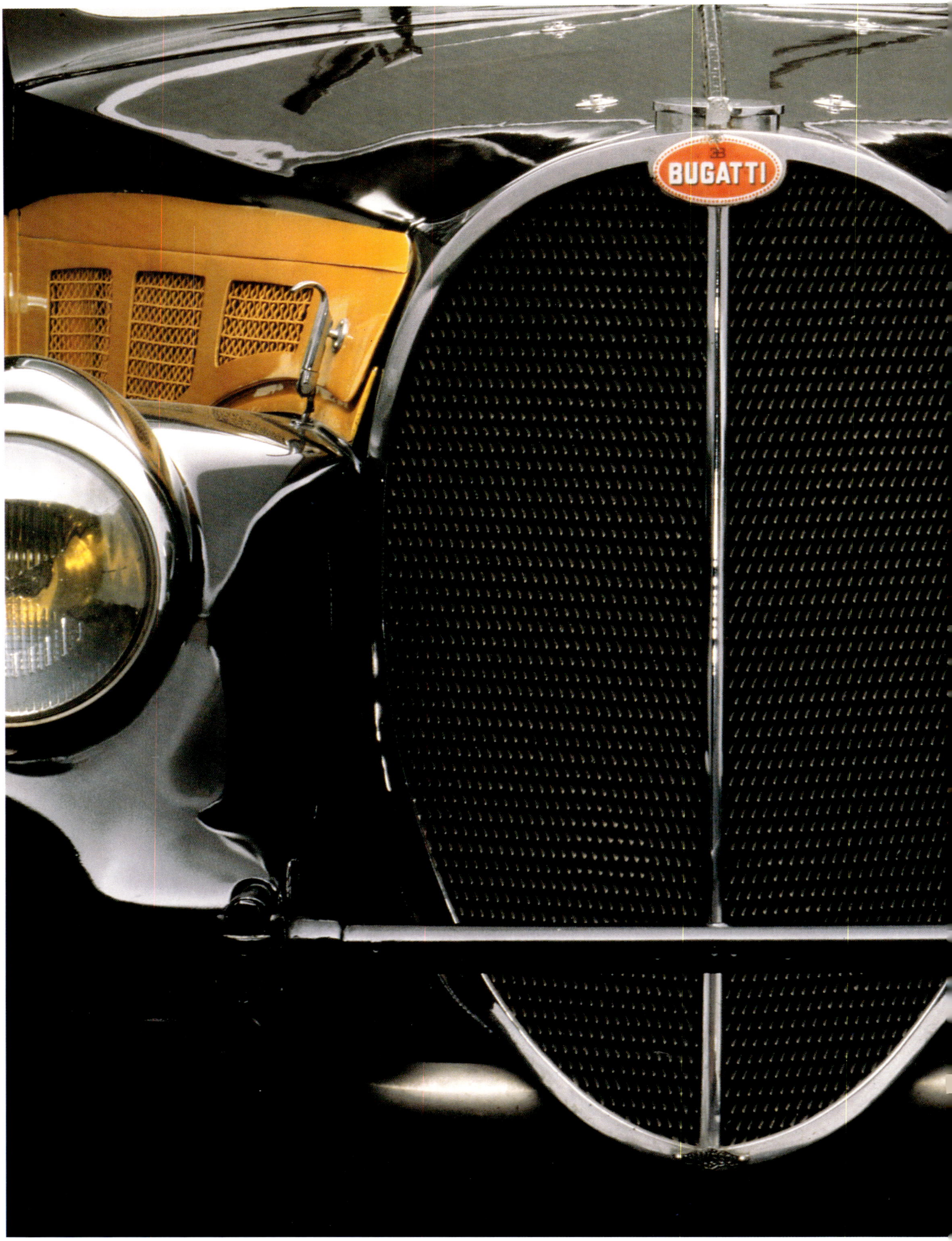
BUGATTI

EDITORIAL

When in the immediate post-war years Pierre Marco, the general manager of the Molsheim works, found himself faced with the impossible challenge of reviving Bugatti's industrial fortunes, the problems confronting him were numerous, complex and insurmountable. The damage caused by the war and the economic and social problems of the period were compounded by the loss of Ettore, the irreplaceable moving spirit of the marque, who died in Paris on 21 August, 1947. His son Jean, the ideal heir to the Bugatti legend and an unforgettable master of style, had died in tragic circumstances eight years earlier. He was testing a competition car in August, 1939, when he was forced to make a desperate, doomed attempt to avoid colliding with and killing an incautious cyclist. In order to protect the jobs of the workers, many of whom were survivors of the Soviet prison camps, the Molsheim workshops concentrated on the maintenance of helicopter components, whilst other engineering projects were set up on behalf of third parties. But in the absence of the creative spark and the innovative drive provided by the family dynasty the projects never flourished, and the Bugatti name was heard of only in relation to memories of its glorious tradition. Whilst the legendary Molsheim thoroughbreds were fading into a long and inevitable period of lethargy, on the other side of the channel a beautiful new and exotic flower going by the sensual and evocative name of Lotus was about to blossom. Lotus was the pet name of the fiancée of a young RAF pilot, Anthony Colin Bruce Chapman, who used it in the early fifties when he created what was to become one of the most technologically advanced British car manufacturers of the post-war years. Belonging to different eras and generations, Ettore Bugatti and Colin Chapman never met face to face. Had they done so there could have a symbolic passing on of the torch of technological progress as testimony to the continuity of an ideal. The same genius, the same innovative vigour and the same desire for style and perfection were constant themes running through all the projects undertaken by both men. The modern car which, even in ordinary every day use, allows us to sample the subtle pleasure of driving in perfect safety owes much to their fundamental and irreplaceable contribution of passion and genius. Today, thanks to the will and entrepreneurial intuition of Romano Artioli, the destinies, objectives and automotive dreams of the two companies have finally been united. Together, Bugatti and Lotus have the opportunity of reviving with renewed strength a conception of the sporting car in which technology is in perfect harmony with the precision and passion of craft-based production of the very highest quality. Leaving aside the economic, industrial and social aspects of the deal, this merger can hardly fail to stimulate a significant and sophisticated degree of synergy between these two glorious European car manufacturers. Our very best wishes go to both Bugatti and Lotus. Ettore and Colin are undoubtedly cheering you on from above. When backed by true ability and great enthusiasm, the spirit of innovation in all fields of human creativity will never be dimmed.

Business strategy

BUGATTI AND LOTUS: LOVE AND MARRIAGE

In this first-hand account by the President of Bugatti Automobili, the motivations, the genesis and the behind-the-scenes stories of a business deal which will have significant repercussions on the current automotive scene and future developments within the industry.

BY ROMANO ARTIOLI

I have to admit that I've gone back on my word with Renata, but I would like to meet the man who could have resisted the temptation I found myself facing. I was closely following the story of the management buy-out at Lotus, and when it appeared that the negotiations with GM had stalled I asked permission to step in, having previously received the go-ahead from Bugatti International SAH. Renata had made me promise that with the establishment of the Bugatti project I would have quit taking on new challenges and dedicated myself to the revival and development of this great marque. Day by day, in fact, Bugatti continues to demonstrate its great strength and unmatched world-wide appeal. But the undreamed of opportunity to unite and protect these two great names proved irresistible. Bugatti and Lotus have between them made a remarkable contribution to the development and progress of the automobile with a series of innovations and patents that would be the envy of all the other manufacturers put together, and their combined rolls of racing honours constitutes the most impressive competition pedigree in automotive history. I am sure that you will agree that my betrayal was justified by such mitigating circumstances as to merit Renata's forgiveness. But now let's go back to the beginning and let you in on the story's magical moments. On 1 June we were invited to GM Europe's Zurich offices which had been charged with the handling of the Lotus sale. Our party comprised myself, our Vice-President Mario Barbieri, who followed each step of the negotiations with great skill, our legal representative Enrico Castellani and our tireless assistant Karen Angus who, on top of her normal work, found herself suddenly submerged by a whirlwind of translations and meetings to organize. Miraculously she managed not only to survive the ordeal, but also to keep perfect track of every last detail of the operation. Our staff was later strengthened with the arrival of Renzo Magnabosco, the man responsible for dealing with all the financial details of the operation, with the addition of the expert English lawyer Andrew Jordan, and above all with the entrance into action of a wonderful man who provided us with an extraordinary example of strength of will and self-denial which at once moved and encouraged us. This was Tim Sweeting of Price Waterhouse, a man of 42 and a real

Above, the historic moment of the signing of the Bugatti-Lotus deal. In the foreground, from the left, Jean Marc Borel, Scott Mackie, Romano Artioli and Mario Barbieri. Behind, from the left, Geoffrey Perry, Andrew Pike, Anthony Loring, Ray Krause, Tim Sweeting, Pedro Farah, Wilfred Mannert, Mark James, Andrew Jordan and Sandra Humphrey. On the facing page, the press conference at Norwich, Romano Artioli alongside Her Royal Highness Gabriella Von Habsburg and Lord Raglan, President of the Bugatti Owners Club.

pillar of strength who was tragically diagnosed as suffering from a grave illness during the course of our work. In spite of the drastic treatment to which he was subjected, he insisted on following each detail of the complex deal, in a demonstration of great dedication and self-sacrifice, until a definitive conclusion had been reached. We would like to dedicate this great success to him too. I must confess that my heart was beating a little faster than normal when I climbed the stairs at GM and shook the hand of Lou Hughes, President of the European operation. My mind went back to when, at twenty-five years of age, I became an Opel dealer and later the Italian distributor for General Motors USA. I enjoyed great success thanks to a marque which has given me much from both a professional and economic point of view, but which above all allowed me to establish the important and valuable international contacts which have proved indispensable in the realization of new projects and in the extension of my horizons. I was also responsible for developing a sporting programme for GM that enjoyed great success and launched the competition career of the little 1900 cc Opel GT which even managed to beat no lesser machines than the Porsches, but that is another story.

The negotiations with GM began with an exchange of documentation and visits during which the heads of the automotive colossus fielded an imposing battery of international lawyers and experts that made our Bugatti team appear very modest! At least in this way the true proportions of our two concerns were represented: today GM is one of the world's largest corporations with over 800,000 people on the pay-roll whilst we number just 200. As I saw things the negotiations lasted an eternity given that I was itching to launch a number of projects with Lotus; from the point of view of GM, accustomed to far more complicated dealings, it was all over very quickly. It was at 4 o'clock on the morning of 26 August, 1993, in London, that we were finally able to drink a toast to the signing of the contract with the Bugatti champagne that Jean Marc Borel had thoughtfully brought with him. Thus another August went by without any summer holidays. It seems to be a constant theme in my life that the most important events always have to happen in August. They asked me what it felt like to have concluded such a significant deal. My first reaction was that one is so tired of evaluating clauses, cavils, conditions and commitments and of examining thousands

→

Business strategy

upon thousands of documents that the joy in having accomplished something extraordinary disappears. I had already met with this sensation on other occasions during my career and so I was prepared for all the stress: it is something akin to going through a whirlwind romance and arriving at the altar exhausted by all the tension. Later of course what remain are the memories of the happy moments and the great satisfaction of having achieved something special. Just like a father who wants a good husband for his daughter, GM naturally wanted to ensure the best possible future for Lotus. In Bugatti it has found an ideal partner capable of developing, understanding and supporting a marque with such fine traditions. The potential for synergy and the numerous opportunities for cooperation are such as to be of significant benefit to both Bugatti and Lotus. Above all the greatest care will be taken to avoid any modification to the concepts of limited scale production and niche marketing characteristic of both marques. Those manufacturers of exclusive luxury goods who have deviated from this strategy during the good times in the search for bigger fish to fry are now paying the price. In contrast we now have the opportunity to launch new ranges of products for Lotus's traditional sporting clientele. This policy will not interfere in any way with the Bugatti programme which will continue to concentrate on an exclusive product of the very highest quality. My past experiences have taught me that it is unwise to offer the same marque to clients of different backgrounds, tastes, cultures and financial means due to the risk of alienating one or the other groups and in the end of damaging the marque. The image of the product is, in fact, closely linked to the image of its clientele, and this represents a very serious and incurable problem for all car manufacturers. In our case, however, there will be no ambiguity as the two marques will maintain their independent identities and clienteles, their respective products being conceived and produced in different factories and for different clients. They will both benefit from significant technical experience, ideas, styles, methods, suppliers, laboratories, safety systems and a pool of common expertise which should enable more rapid development of new models. The marques' sales networks could also be utilized to mutual advantage - Lotus is well established in the Commonwealth countries and the USA - whilst maintaining discrete marketing strategies. Lotus has another ace up its sleeve which is extremely important today, and will become ever more so in relation to the developments in the automotive world of the near future. We are, in fact, in the middle of a revolution in which the rules of the game which previously left manufacturers with the sole task of producing vehicles that satisfied market demands are changing rapidly. Nowadays the problems of environmental pollution, the need to protect public health, the demands for individual safety, the problems related to the disposal of waste products and so on are gradually becoming the subject of legislation applying to everybody and in every country throughout the world. The automobile has thus got to change, and change now. Bugatti, and now Lotus, as independent companies free to collaborate with all other parties, have the chance to play an extremely important role by proposing new features to the major manufacturers as well as to new firms looking for an outlet on the market. Crisis or no crisis, the automotive sector is still very attractive because the statistics still show an annual production total of over 45 million units. Lotus is a leader in the automotive engineering sector and the projects that it is now free to develop for other clients, on top of its existing contracts with GM, guarantee it a prosperous future. And this not all by any means, as new patents are on the horizon directly deriving from the collaboration between Bugatti and Lotus, with both firms working hard to satisfy the restrictive new normatives. Thus

In the photo above, the Lotus Managing Director Adrian Palmer (left) the President of Bugatti Automobili, Romano Artioli and the President of Bugatti International, Jean Mark Borel pose alongside the super-fast and sophisticated Esprit, current star of the Lotus line-up.

there is plenty of work to be done; the potential of both firms is enormous, certainly far greater than their paper values might suggest. We shall go into the facts, figures and forecasts in the next edition of the magazine. Going back to our story once again; a couple of days after the historic completion of the contract we visited the Lotus works to meet the personnel and the management team and to shed a little light on the initial plans for the future. I have reason to believe that the visit was a success as the journalists lying in wait to interview the workers in the heat of the moment, to get an idea of the mood "following the acquisition of the factory by the Italians", heard from the Lotus workers that "it couldn't be better, as being bought by Bugatti is an honour", that "at last there are projects to develop", and that "they would be able to demonstrate what they are capable of". They have already demonstrated these capabilities and no mistake! In the space of 15 days, working overtime and without asking for a penny, they cleaned and reorganized the factory from top to bottom, repainted the buildings, renovated the workshops and machinery, tidied up the surrounding grounds and organized the presentation ceremony. The ceremony was held in the presence of journalists from all over the world, dealers, VIPs, the Lotus clubs and the British Bugatti Owners Club. Furthermore, the factory was opened to the public for the first time in many years.

I have to say that all this genuinely moved me, and I was overjoyed by the confirmation that Hethel was still manned by a skilled team with a great will to work. And we will not be slow in providing them with the opportunity to do so as the projects for the relaunching of Lotus are well in hand and will soon be set in motion. After having seen the Lotus premises so immaculate and having discovered the enthusiasm with which the personnel work, the head of the GM delegation, Scott Mackie, a tough but very fair negotiator, said that had he discovered it earlier he would never have sold the company.

We were thus able to celebrate the anniversary of the birth of Ettore Bugatti in a way that would have been unthinkable a few short months earlier, with two sensational coups for an enterprise of our size: the presentation of the EB 112 Sports Saloon at Geneva and the acquisition of the Lotus Group. Moreover,we had two more pleasant surprises to dedicate to Ettore: the prize for the "World's Most Beautiful Saloon" presented to the EB 112 at Milan by the Automobilia jury, and the prize for the "Grand Turismo most appreciated by the German readers of Sport Auto" awarded to the EB 110. The story certainly does not end here as for us just as it was for Ettore Bugatti, "every objective attained is but the point of departure for new, more demanding horizons".

Talent
head-to-head

PARALLEL LIVES

Ettore Bugatti and Colin Chapman were the protagonists in two enthralling stories that were less far removed from one another than the years separating them might suggest. Two exemplary philosophies: the automobile as objet d'art, and racing as a laboratory for the future.

BY GIANNI CANCELLIERI

Anthony Colin Bruce Chapman died on 16 December, 1982, one hundred and one years, three months and a day after the birth of Ettore Arco Isidoro Bugatti (15 September, 1881). Nevertheless, the career of France's greatest Italian almost overlapped with the beginnings of the Englishman's. When Bugatti died on 21 August, 1947, Chapman (born 19 May, 1928) was nineteen years old and, in a shed behind his fiancée and future wife Hazel Patricia William's house, working on the transformation of a 1930 Austin Seven which was to be a successful trials car known as the Lotus Mk 1.

The origins of the two figures were very different. The Bugattis were artists, Carlo, the father, a distinguished cabinet-maker and silversmith, was the creator of fantastic furniture with oriental influences; Carlo's sister Luigia married the famous Divisionist painter Giovanni Segantini, a fellow student of Carlo's at Milan's Accademia di Brera; Ettore's younger brother Rembrandt was not a painter but a sculptor of great talent. Ettore himself studied painting and sculpture and also enrolled at the Accademia di Brera, but he was to make a decisive

Above, in the photo dating back to the immediate pre-war years alongside the title, Ettore Bugatti at work at his drawing board. To those who asked if he was a qualified engineer he replied "I never had the time". Left, Colin Chapman in the early sixties saluting one of the many Formula 1 victories of his protegé Jim Clark.

about-turn in favour of mechanical engineering after being "enlightened" by a trial run in a Prinetti & Stucchi powered tricycle when he was little more than adolescent. "I immediately realised that that tricycle could be modified" he was to write in his memoirs.

The Chapmans were a more modest family. Colin's father Stanley owned and ran a bar which allowed the family to keep their heads above water during the dark years of the Second World War and to cultivate notions of social improvement for their only child. Colin went to university to read engineering in late 1945, graduating in 1948 with a specialization in structural calculus. In the meantime he had started small-scale used car trading but soon had to give it up as unprofitable. He then turned to the car conversion work mentioned earlier: an activity destined to lead to him becoming a fully fledged car constructor within a few years.

Difficult beginnings, the lack of capital and the need to borrow were common themes in the stories of both Bugatti and

→

Right, Graham Hill racing in 1968 with the Lotus 49. The single-seater equipped with the Ford-Cosworth three-litre V8 was characterized by a large rear wing mounted directly onto the wheel hubs.
In the photo above, a front view of the legendary Bugatti Royale Roadster. This elegant car lacked headlights as its owner, Armand Edsers, never drove at night.

In the photo on the left, two generations of Bugatti "Tanks" heads-to-head. Top, Ernst Friederich with his mechanic at the ACF Grand Prix in 1923 with the Type 32. Below, the Type 57 Tanks of Wimille, Benoist and Veyron lined up on the occasion of the French Grand Prix at Monthlèry in 1936.

Chapman, although the plots were to develop along different lines. Both were precocious talents and both worked for others before setting up their respective firms. At seventeen Bugatti joined Prinetti & Stucchi and was actively involved in the production of the first cars, rapidly learning through hands-on experience all the secrets of the manufacturing process, and making personal contributions in various areas. Following university and the Lotus Mk 1, Chapman carried out his military service in the RAF before joining the British Aluminium Company. However, night and day, all he was thinking about in his spare time was new cars. When you come down to it he too was self-taught. At university he had certainly learnt how to calculate material strengths and whilst studying for his pilot's license he had looked at the basics of aeronautical engineering, intellectual baggage that undoubtedly found some application, but actual manufacturing was something he learnt for himself on a trial and error basis as he perfected the techniques with implacable determination. A preoccupation with perfection an inexhaustible innovative drive were also common to both. Bugatti achieved a degree of success in some of the earliest motor races aboard Prinetti & Stucchi tricycles he prepared and designed himself (in particular one powered by two De Dion-Bouton engines) but his greatest efforts were directed towards an entirely new car. He was still working for Prinetti & Stucchi but the company were not convinced by his avant-garde ideas although they allowed him to go it alone.

Talent head-to-head

Above, the unmistakable, functional form of the Bugatti Type 53 from 1931, the first car featuring permanent four-wheel drive. Below, the Type 59 from 1934, considered by some to be the most beautiful Grand Prix Bugatti.

Bugatti succeeded in persuading Count Gulinelli di Ferrara to finance the production of his first complete car. It was powered by one of the rare early four-cylinder engines and featured compact two-seater coachwork. Presented at the "International Sports Exhibition" at Milan in May, 1901, it was admired and won awards. Bugatti, not yet twenty-one years of age, acquired a degree of international fame and never looked back.

The young Chapman also competed in trials, a form of off-road rallying, and on the track in his Lotus models which from the very outset presented some of engineering traits which were to become features of all the marque's cars: the stiffening of the chassis with the minimum increase in weight, the lowering of the centre of gravity and independent suspension. All of these elements provided advantages in terms of handling and thus a chance to prevail over cars of the same or even larger cylinder capacities. It was this that made the Lotuses winners and allowed them to be produced in small production runs. Chapman formed Lotus Engineering in 1951, but it was not until 1955 - at twenty-seven years of age - that he dedicated himself entirely to his vocation.

The Bugatti vocation had undeniably wider horizons and encompassed a global

→

Left, Colin Chapman personally testing the Lotus 49 at Hethel. This was the first Formula 1 single-seater to be fitted with the Ford-Cosworth DFV.

Above, the Austrian World Champion Jochen Rindt driving the Lotus 72 in 1970. This car was characterized by a perfect wedge shape, a triplane rear wing, torsion bar suspension and in-board disc brakes.

conception of car manufacturing. At first Ettore put his talent at the disposition of a number of European manufacturers: De Dietrich of Niederbronn, Mathis of Strasbourg and Deutz of Cologne. It was actually at Cologne that "le Pur Sang", the first car to carry his name, was created by Bugatti working at night in his cellar. In 1909 when Ettore was twenty-eight he founded the company destined to bring him eternal fame.

Once they had started working on their own accounts, Bugatti and Chapman were like two volcanoes in a permanent state of eruption. The fruits of their labours were so abundant that there simply is not the space here to describe them all. Nevertheless I will try to sketch out a kind of anthology that summarizes two extraordinary chapters in automotive history.

In contrast to Chapman, Bugatti was a great engine designer and his entire oeuvre bears testimony to the fact, from the small, light four-cylinder 1.3-litre unit with overhead valves fitted to the type 13 to the immortal dynasty of eight-cylinder units prepared in a dozen configurations from the minuscule 1092 cc version fitted to the Type 36 to the monumental 12,763 cc unit of the Royale (Type 41), by way of the 2- and 2.2-litre Grand Prix engines of the Type 35, the principal conquerer of a roll of competition honours that between 1924 and 1927 alone numbered 1,851 victories. But alongside the competition activities and cars Bugatti made a virtual cult out of the search for beauty combined with functionality in forms. The automobile was for him a true work of art. As Conway has written, his Grand Turismo cars, with coachwork masterfully designed by his son Jean, "rivalled for elegance and surpassed in functionality those of the

Great champions past and present drove the cars created by Colin Chapman. In the photo above, Ayrton Senna with the Lotus 98T in 1985. Below, the English constructor in action in 1955 with his beloved and shapely 1100 cc Mark 9.

greatest Italian and French coachbuilders". Chapman on the other hand concentrated on racing.

He did of course create a range of avant-garde GT's (Elan, Europa, Elite, Esprit, Eclat) as well as an unusual sports car, the Lotus Seven, presented in 1957 and still built under licence by Caterham. However, year by year, his interest was focused ever more exclusively on competition cars (Enzo Ferrari was the same in this respect), cars which brought him worldwide success and fame, as well as place in the history of engineering as one of its greatest innovators.

These are his most precious "jewels": the Lotus 25, the single-seater that brought monocoque construction to Formula One; the Lotus 38, the car that triumphed at Indianapolis; the Lotus 49, the first car to achieve success with the legendary Ford-Cosworth DFV eight-cylinder engine; the four-wheel drive Lotus 64; the Lotus 77 with variable geometry suspension; the ground effects Lotus 78; the Lotus 88 with its twin carbonfibre chassis...

In twenty-five years of participation (1958-1982) in the Formula 1 World Championship under the guidance of Colin Chapman, Lotus collected no less than 13 titles (7 manufacturers' Championships, and 6 Drivers': Jim Clark (twice), Graham Hill, Jochen Rindt, Emerson Fittipaldi and Mario Andretti), 72 victories, 88 pole positions and 63 fastest laps. Chapman had developed the Lotus 92 equipped with active suspension for the 1983 season, but was never to see it take to the track. The news of his death due to a heart attack in the early hours of the morning on 16 December, 1982, broke during the car's first testing session on the Snetterton circuit.

He was fifty-four years old and still had the will and desire to go on translating his philosophy - that racing improves the breed - into a practical reality. □

Events
CLOSE ENCOUNTERS BETWEEN TECHNOLOGY AND STYLE

Ettore Bugatti and Colin Chapman were brought together at the Bologna Motor Show to illustrate automotive development through the histories and creations of their celebrated marques.

BY ROBERTO MERLO

As far as the general public is concerned, Ettore Bugatti and Colin Chapman symbolically met for the first time last year at Bologna, in Hall 21 of the 12th edition of the Motor Show.
A significant and emblematic coming together marking an extremely important event: the passage of an ideal from one great and unforgettable automotive genius to another. Bugatti and Lotus, the companies created by Ettore and Colin, decided to jointly stage a major technical-historical display providing enthusiasts with an overview of the companies' distinguished pasts (during which innovations of fundamental importance to the development of automotive engineering were introduced), the entrepreneurial reality of the present and the future prospects for two marques that as a logical consequence of the recent agreements have decided to follow a policy of parallel development.
Bugatti International S.A.H. acquired the

In the photos on these pages, views of the large hall set up by Bugatti and Lotus at the 12th Bologna Motor Show. Dream cars of the past and present were placed in evocative settings.

entire parcel of Lotus Group shares from General Motors on 26 August, 1993. The Group comprises three companies, Lotus Cars, Lotus Engineering and Lotus Cars USA. As the spokesmen of both parties explained, this acquisition has been made on the understanding that the autonomy and identity of the marques will be respected, with the two firms quite rightly remaining separate entities.
The benefits of the union will be evident in the very near future in the form of the fascinating potential for synergy on both technological and commercial levels.
An entire hall at the Motor Show 1993 was dedicated to this extraordinary compound of style, technology and innovation which has succeeded in enlightening automotive culture for decades.
The Bugatti-Lotus stand was not designed

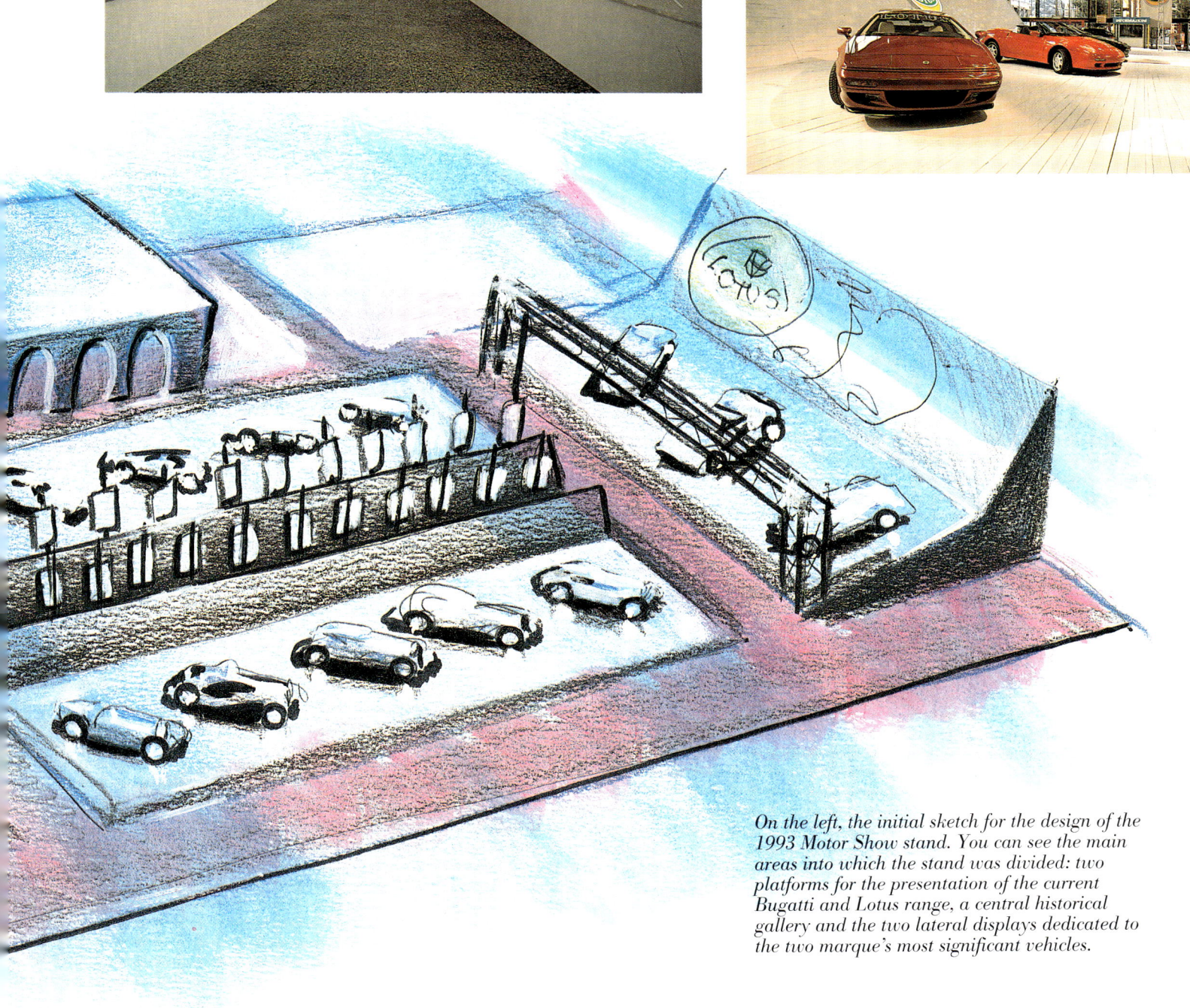

On the left, the initial sketch for the design of the 1993 Motor Show stand. You can see the main areas into which the stand was divided: two platforms for the presentation of the current Bugatti and Lotus range, a central historical gallery and the two lateral displays dedicated to the two marque's most significant vehicles.

Events

as a museum.

The efficiently accomplished aim was simple: to provide an youthful public with a condensed history of the two companies, to illustrate in an immediate and concrete way the problems that Bugatti and Lotus have tackled during their respective eras, their sporting, technological and entrepreneurial triumphs and the innovative drive and personal charisma of their two founders.

The key to the display was the creation of a gallery in heart of the exhibition hall, within which the parallel histories of the two marques were unfolded.

Through a series of documents, previously unseen photographs and technical drawings, Bugatti and Lotus offered the visitors to the Motor Show an account of their historical significance and the innovations which they have introduced to the automotive world.

Two vehicle displays were set up outside the gallery with the historical evolution of the Bugatti marque on one side and that of Lotus on the other. At either end of the large hall were areas dedicated to the two marques' current models, whilst the Ettore Bugatti firm furnished the reception area with a richly suggestive and comprehensive display of exclusive articles from its "Bugatti emotion" collection.

LOTUS MK 6
In its early days Lotus occupied a small building in Tottenham Lane. There was not enough space to build complete cars but with a stroke of genius Colin Chapman came up with a sports car to be sold in kit form. This was the Mk 6 and enjoyed great success.

LOTUS 11
Colin Chapman felt that the extremely light and powerful Coventry Climax fire pump engine could work in a racing car. He chose it for the Lotus 11, a car with shapely bodywork and a spaceframe chassis. In 1956 the 1100 and 1500 cc Elevens dominated the British tracks and also made their presence felt in Europe. In 1957 a 750 cc 11 won the performance index at Le Mans.

LOTUS 14 ELITE
The plastic car is still science fiction today, never mind back in 1957. Yet in that year Lotus introduced the Elite which featured a fibreglass chassis and bodyshell. The only metal components were the windscreen frame and a suspension sub-frame. Its strengths were its lightness (643 kg) and its aerodynamics. It reached a top speed of 175 km/h with a 75 hp engine.

LOTUS 22
Inclining the engine by 30° and forcing the driver to adopt a semi-prone position, Chapman produced an extremely low, shapely and successful Formula Junior car. Peter Arundell's 22, an 18-time winner in 1962, was so quick that the journalist Richard Von Frankemberg wagered that its engine was over-sized. The unit was dismantled and the hack's lack of faith cost him a pretty penny.

LOTUS 23
This was Lotus' most successful sports racer. The chassis, suspension and engine were all derived from those of the Formula Junior 22. Its reasonable price (£ 1650 in kit form) exceptional performance great handling made it a popular choice among privateers.

LOTUS 26 ELAN
The Lotus Elite was a failure on economic terms - it cost the earth. Lotus made amends with the Elan. Chapman mounted a Ford-Lotus 1500 cc engine on an unusual steel backbone chassis with only the bodyshell in plastic. The Elan was an excellent road car as well as a competitive racer... so much so that the Japanese Mazda firm have produced virtually a carbon copy for the nineties.

LOTUS 28 CORTINA
The transplantation of the Lotus Elite's twin-cam engine transformed the placid Ford Cortina into a raging beast. The unforgettable Jim Clark and Sir John Withmore, leader of the Alan Mann Racing team took it by the scruff of its neck on the European Touring Car circuits. In epic duels against the Alfa Romeo Giulia Ti Super and the BMW 1800 Tisa, the Lotus Cortina's weight advantage was the key to many victories.

LOTUS 46 EUROPA
Colin Chapman turned around the drivetrain of a front-wheel drive saloon to produce an economical mid-engined sports car, the Europa. The very slippery coachwork (Cd = 0.29) made up for the Renault 16 engine's scanty power output. The final price was rather too high to make it a truly economical proposition and the Europa finished its career as a racer fitted with a Ford-Cosworth engine.

LOTUS 79 F1
The 79 was the first true ground effects car and carried Mario Andretti to the World Championship in 1978. With the discovery of ground effects Colin Chapman gave an extra element of safety and driveability to even everyday cars which actually increases as speeds rise.

BUGATTI TYPE 35
The Type 35 is the archetypal Bugatti and it was with this model that the Molsheim constructor made a definitive impact. The car boasts a magnificent roll of honour comprising over 2,000 victories. Among its technical innovations were: light alloy wheels (the world's first), the faired underbody and the well judged wheelbase dimension, still used on current sports cars.

BUGATTI TYPE 40
There was never a budget model Bugatti, but at least this model was not stratospherically expensive. The secret lay in the cunning use of Bugatti parts bin components. The 1.5-litre engine came from the 37, an the gearbox and rear axle from the Type 38 B. It appealed to the ladies as it was lively but did not require the skills of a G.P. driver.

BUGATTI TYPE 43
A single-seater for four people is the philosophy behind the Type 43 which used the supercharged eight-cylinder 2.2-litre engine from the Type 35. Powerful, very fast and manoeuvrable, it was a car that could be used to the full. Its extremely high price did nothing to prevent its success. It was especially attractive with bodywork designed and built in-house like this Torpedo.

BUGATTI TYPE 46
Ettore Bugatti conceived the Royale for crowned heads of state, but no King ever dared buy it. Karol of Rumania actually feared a revolution if his people ever found out its cost. Bugatti made amends with the Type 46, a magnificent, elegant car with much of the appeal of the Royale including the beautiful ventilated alloy wheels. Luxury and performance were never so happily combined.

BUGATTI TYPE 56
Ettore Bugatti used his horse or this extremely simple electric car to get around his factory. The Type 56's gig-like bodywork made it remarkably accessible and it could carry two people. It featured tiller steering and a stop-go lever. The extremely quiet engine was rear-mounted.

BUGATTI TYPE 57 ATLANTIC
In 1936 Jean Bugatti, Ettore's favourite son, designed the mechanicals and bodywork of the fabulous 57 Atlantic, admirably tempering the notably innovative character of the twin-cam eight-cylinder engine and revolutionary aerodynamic body with composed and elegant styling in the best Molsheim traditions.

Bugatti's technological innovations have had an influence over decades of automotive history. Back in 1914 16-valve engines had already been introduced, whilst cast alloy wheels made there debuts in 1924. In 1932 Bugatti introduced four-wheel drive with three differentials. These are all features which have yet to be universally adopted.

Lotus 11

Lotus 14 Elite

Lotus 79

Bugatti Type 35

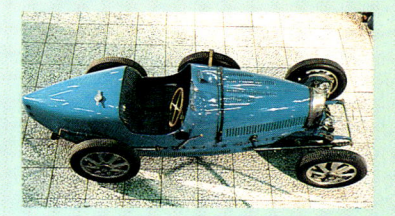

Bugatti Type 43

Bugatti Type 46

Bugatti Type 57

Past and present

THE NEW BUGATTI ARCHITECTURE

The architectonic elements and the styles linking the Molsheim workshops with the new Campogalliano factory and the Ora Styling Centre. Surroundings and services on a human scale designed to enhance the quality of the working conditions and the end product. Harmonies, colours and forms that are setting trends.

BY ROBERTO MERLO

Right, an aerial view of the Bugatti Styling Centre at Ora. Below, in the large photo, the fully glazed building designed to house the management offices, the designers and the draughtsmen. On the facing page, above the title, the full extent of the Bugatti Automobili works and, in the centre a period poster with a view of the Molsheim factory.

The German architect Walter Gropius (1883-1969), considered one of the father figures of the industrial architecture of the early twentieth century, was convinced that the "factories of the modern" should not be limited to the clothing of the various productive activities with a more or less rational technological wrapper. As he affirmed in 1913, "the objective is that of creating a worthy form for industrial building which may have an impact on the public whilst at the same time improving the conditions of the worker, providing him not only with light, air and cleanliness, but also the impression of a great entrepreneurial concept". Essentially what Gropius was saying was that workers ought to offered, through the beauty and grandeur of the industrial structures, a means of overcoming the monotony of mechanical factory work. Out of this concept came a tendency to marry art and monumentality

→

in industrial building in order to express those concepts of impetus, dynamism and rigour which, at that time, were features of the organization of labour. The availability of new materials such as steel, glass and later reinforced concrete, which at first seemed incompatible, allowed the development and consolidation of a grandiose and spectacular style of architecture which sprang out of the questionable precept of reviving the pleasure in labour through a purely aesthetic factor. Steel pyramids, glass walls and reinforced concrete arches never actually did succeed in contributing to the improvement of the quality of life within the factory.

Although Ettore Bugatti was undoubtedly well aware of those aesthetic and social upheavals, especially when he was rebuilding and extending the Molsheim workshops after the destruction caused by the First World War, he did not seem to be affected by any desire to express ideas of grandeur through the architectural design of his factory. The Molsheim factory was functional and rational, clean and well lit, surrounded by greenery but at the same time well connected to the road and rail networks. The building style adopted, free of the useless ornamentation, art nouveau decorations or post-romantic symbolism so fashionable in the early twentieth century, appeared rather more domestic than industrial. This was a typical expression of the very "Bugattian" philosophy whereby the whole complex was oriented towards the legitimate needs and expectations of the working man.

As far as Bugatti was concerned, Molsheim was more than just the "factory of his dreams", it was also his home, his extended family. During the prime years of his industrial career, the great Ettore created an intimate personal universe within the Molsheim complex, a universe where art, labour and passion could happily coexist. He had decided to live within the grounds and so had a large private house built at the centre of the tree-filled park. Alongside the house he built stables for the race horses which, after the automobile, were the second great love of his life and a building close by was fitted out as a museum for the sculptures of his brother Rembrandt who had died in 1916. The Bugatti's private area was completed a special distillery for the production of Alsatian brandy and kennels for Ettore's beloved fox terriers. Friends, drivers and important clients were, on the other hand, put up at the Hostellerie du Pur Sang, a small hotel personally run by the family and situated close by the factory. Many visitors to the factory were unable to conceal their amazement. The Molsheim complex was actually one of the most well equipped and sophisticated in the world. It represented not only a centre of high level mechanical engineering, but also the

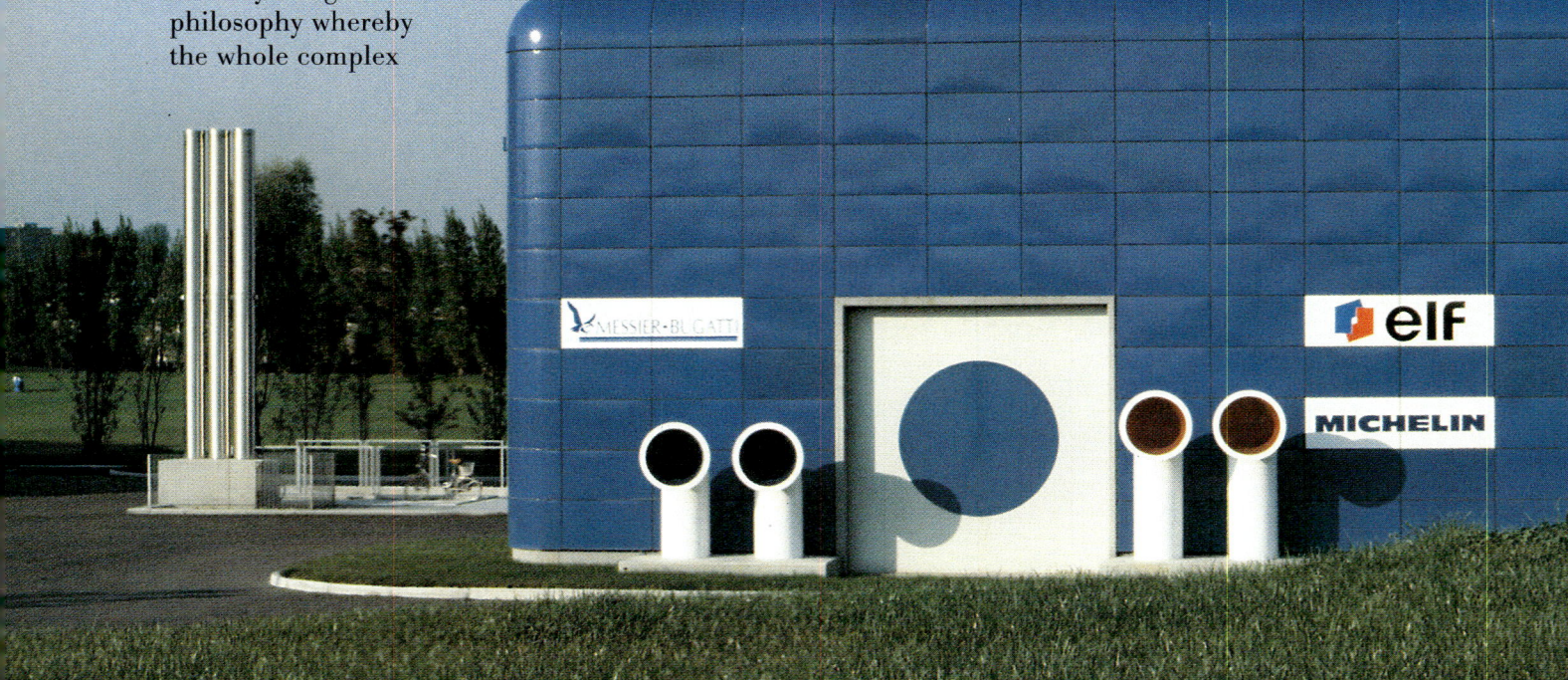

The heart of the Campogalliano establishment, in the photo below, is the characteristic building clad in sheet metal housing the engine testing hall. Above, a period shot of a sixteen-cylinder Bugatti aero engine being bench tested.

thriving, dynamic focal point from which Bugatti projected an exclusive conception and interpretation of the automobile as an expression of art and culture, an object of desire worthy of imagination and emotion. It was the castle, the estate, the principality of the last and enlightened Italian Renaissance gentleman, a miraculous survivor of the era of the industrial revolution. The desire to recreate today the stimuli, the emotions and the spirit of the Molsheim era with new projects and new materials appeared to be an impossible task. The Artiolis, the powers-that-be behind the Bugatti renaissance, have rightly avoided the temptation to produce an ineffectual and counter-productive revival of the past. The respect for and appreciation of history rather than its sterile repetition were, in fact, fundamental elements in the successful strategy employed in relaunching the marque. It was with this in mind that Renata and Romano Artioli briefed their architects, and constantly followed each stage of the construction to ensure that the concept was transformed into form and function. Thus the forms of marque's unique modern buildings are impregnated with the essence of the Bugatti spirit. But is there really a Bugatti style expressed by the architectural qualities of the buildings at Ora and →

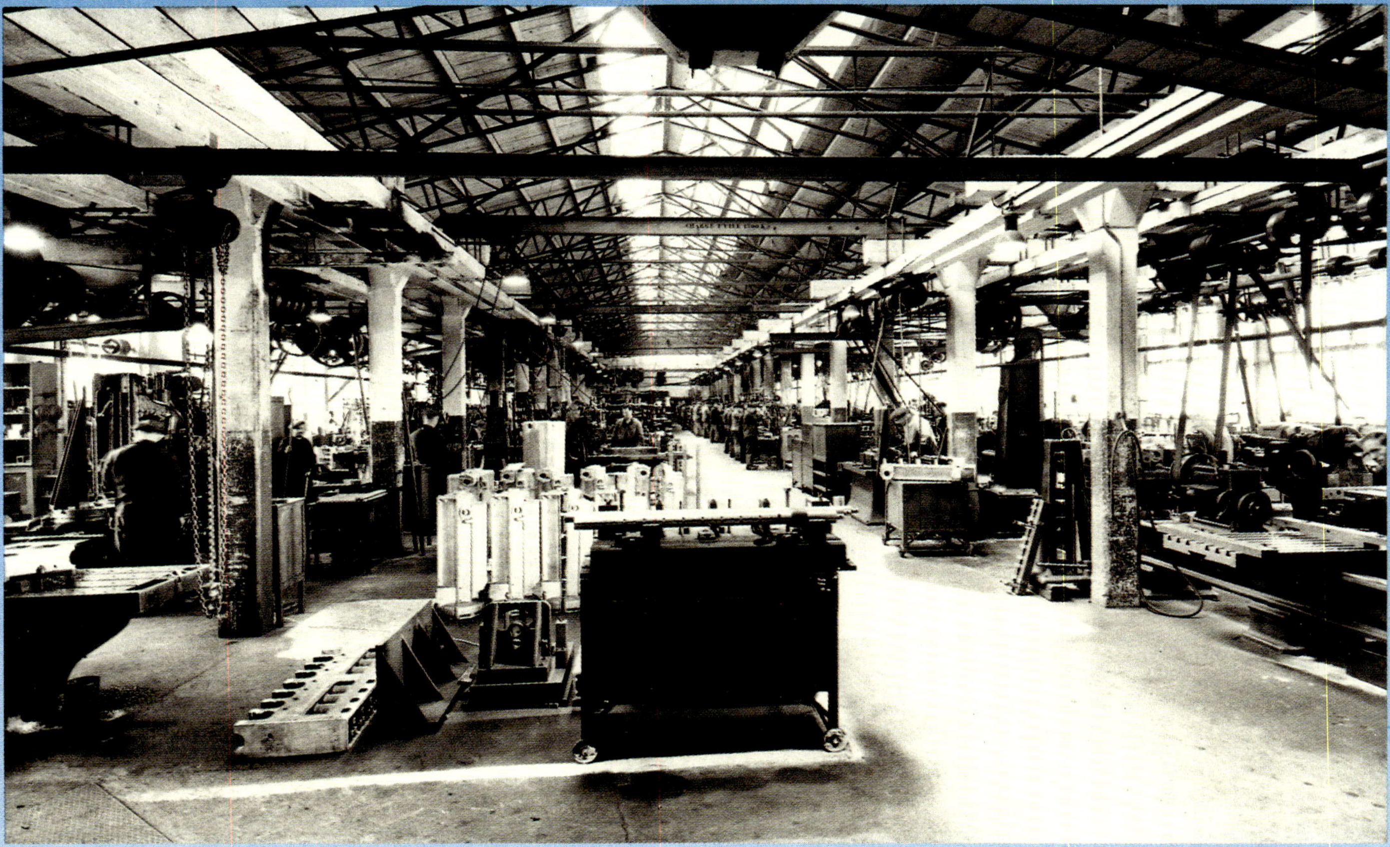

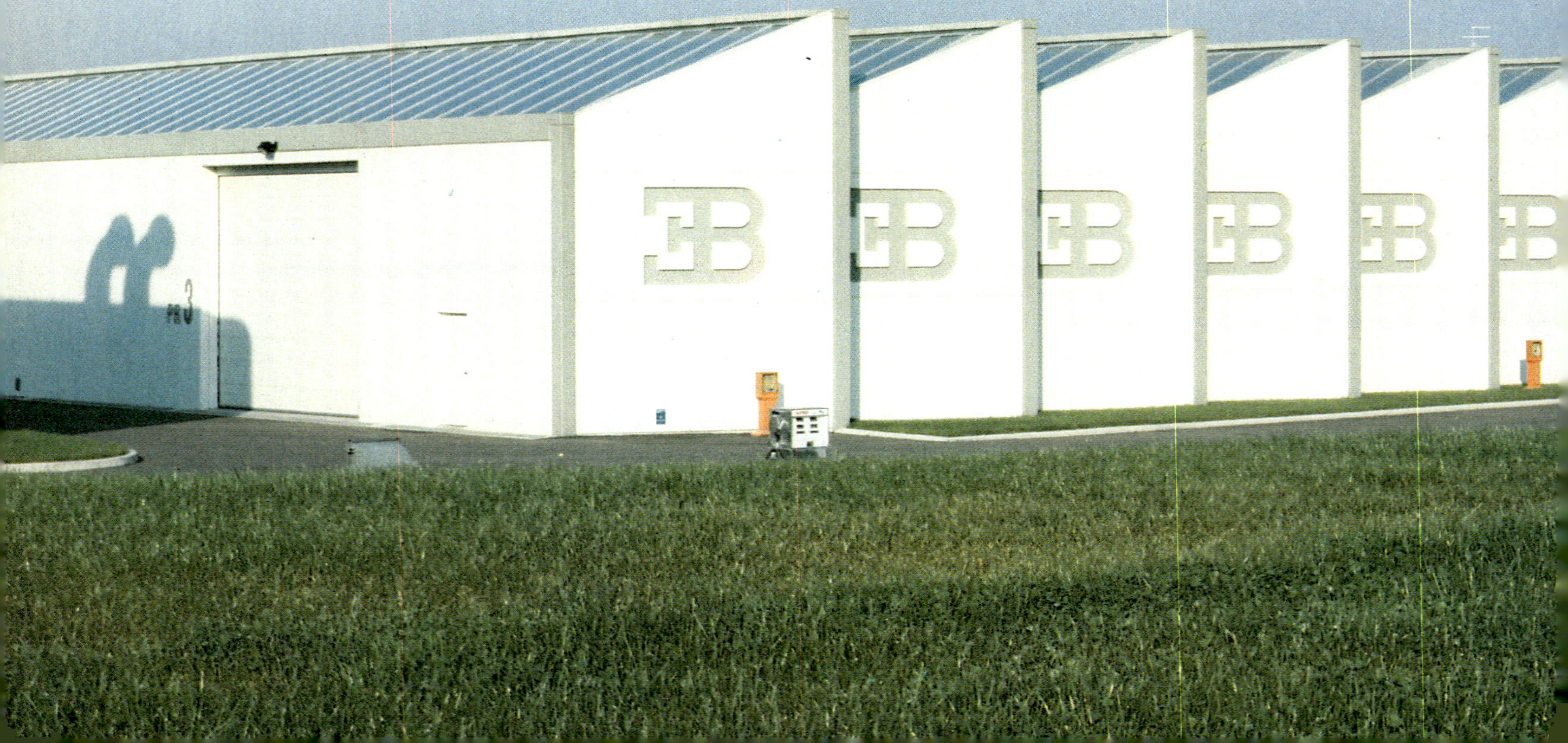

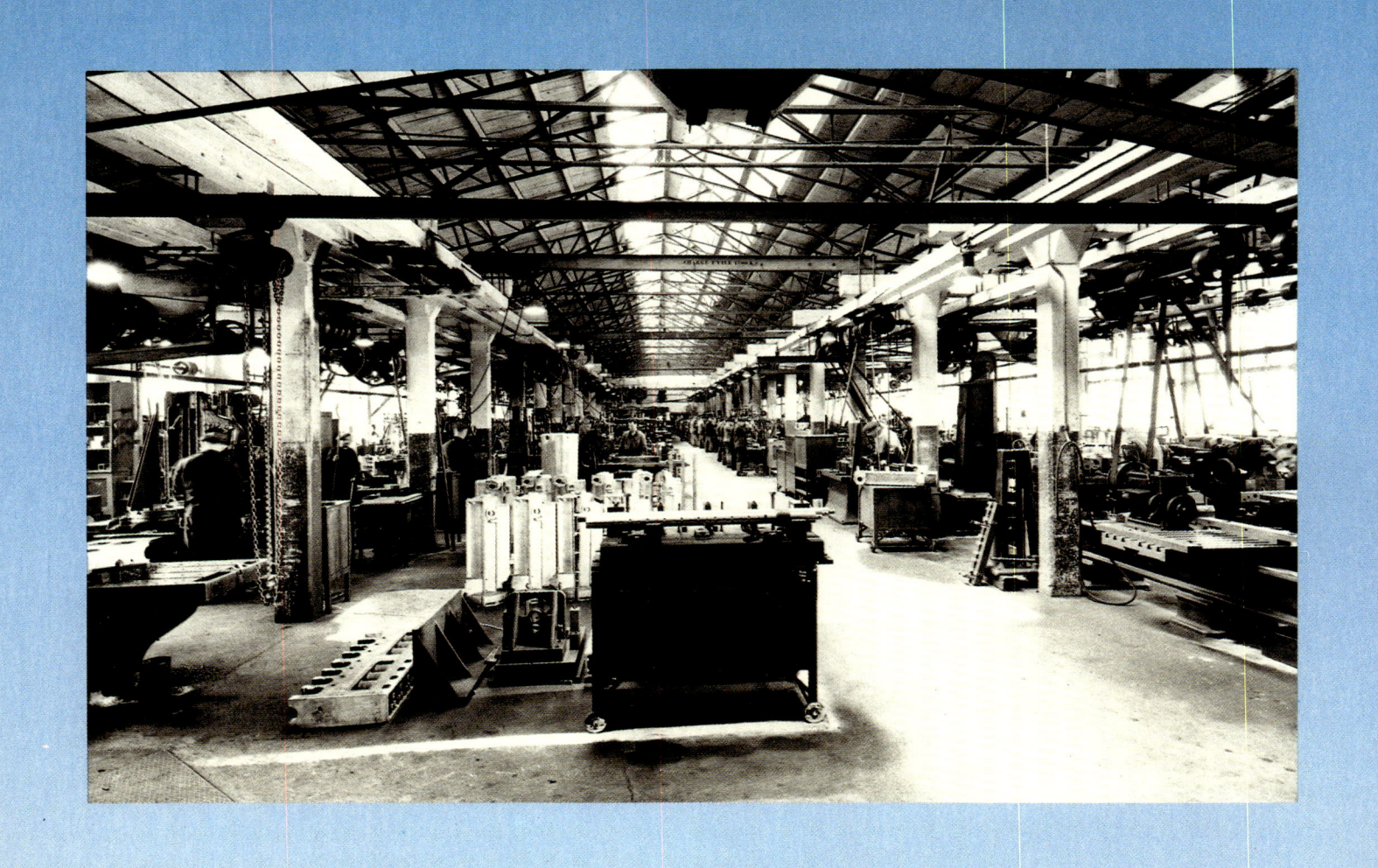

Below, the functional building housing the machine shops and the drivetrain and vehicle assembly lines at Campogalliano. In the photo above, the EB 110 at the end of its luminous and panoramic assembly line. On the facing page, in black and white, a stage in the assembly of the engines in the Molsheim workshops.

Campogalliano? The architect of Bugatti Automobili's Campogalliano works replies, "If by style you mean an aesthetic then I'd say no. If by style you mean a formula, a general philosophy, a method of approach, then yes, I'd say there is. From the aesthetic point of view we're dealing with two diverse realities united, however,

common theme: rationality of design. In substance what was done was to privilege, both at Campogalliano and at Ora, certain rational functions in relation to spaces designed to favour the quality of the working environment. The spaces were planned according to the activities carried out by those who would have to use them. Obviously this has not come about by chance, but stems from the clearly expressed desire of the client who, furthermore, assigned the projects to two different architects."

Another factor that becomes clear as you examine the new Bugatti architecture concerns the simplicity of the structures. A simplicity that is by no means unsophisticated or banal; the materials used both inside and out are, for example, extremely carefully chosen and combined. In the case of the Campogalliano buildings it is only natural to ask whether there really is a link with the past, whether a deliberate architectural reference has been made to the Molsheim workshops. According to Benedini, "Campogalliano and Molsheim are two different things because they were created in two different eras. What I see as a connecting link with the →

On these pages, evocative images of Campogalliano's modern architecture. Right, the design sector, a fully glazed circular building. In the small photo, a view of the administration building. Below, the engine testing centre by moonlight.

past is the concept of 'total design'. Ettore Bugatti was an eclectic genius who defined with extreme precision everything that he produced. Not just a part, but every single element. Thus he always tried to take a global approach to design. For example, the furnishings of the old Bugatti works were produced to special designs, as were many other exterior and interior details, tools and equipment included. During the design phase we adopted this approach. Whilst often using mass produced materials we tried to combine them in unusual ways and to personalize the use of the majority of the prefabricated elements. In all of the structures we have created there is a strong rational, technological element, but there is also a philosophical, idealist component". Part of the office zone at Campogalliano comprises a circular structure, a deliberately chosen form.

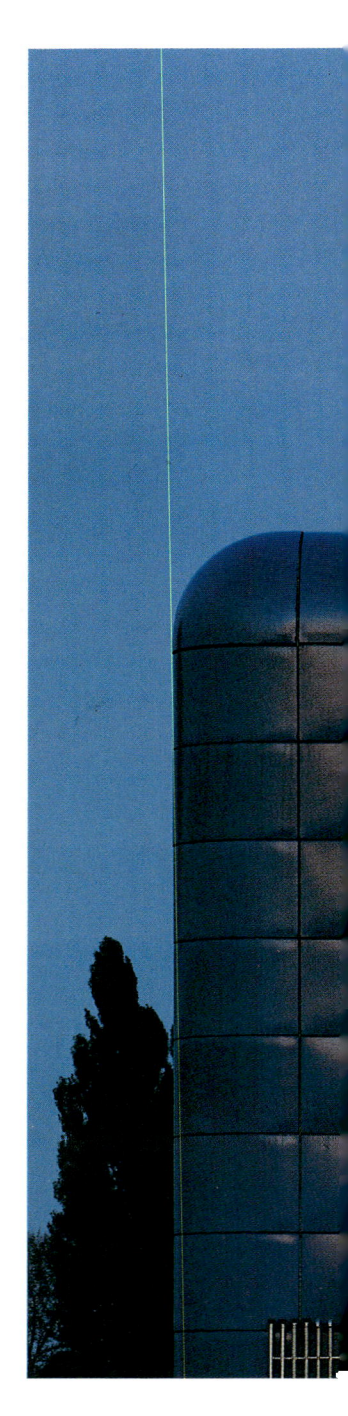

This was the space in which the draughtsmen were to work and the architect has thus taken into consideration the optimum orientation of the light sources. Free of internal walls, this space allows the all draughtsmen's drawing boards to be arranged radially and correctly illuminated. Another interesting building is that housing the engine test benches. In this case the architectural decisions were correlated to the functionality of the building and its particular significance. The engine testing centre is, in fact, the very heart of the factory for a car manufacturer, a key sector that should express vitality, strength and dynamism. This building alone, not the others, within the whole Campogalliano complex has been finished in the typical Bugatti blue. The building's exterior panelling has been produced using a high-tech sheet metal material perfectly in keeping with its function. The sheets have been shaped to produce a building with rounded edges like those of automotive coachwork.

The architectonic features of the buildings used for car production are particularly interesting. "Above all, we took into consideration", continued Benedini, "the people working inside. Working in an industrial building often leads to a loss of

→

contact with reality, often for prolonged periods. In contrast, we wanted to ensure that this contact was maintained. It is only right and proper that rather than being an alienating process labour should be an activity that provides us with strength and satisfaction. We thus decided to open up the building to provide more light and more visual stimulation through a system of staggered 'sheds'. Obviously the surroundings had to be up to scratch; we could hardly leave the external environment a squalid mess of dust, rubble and weeds. We had to create a backdrop that could be enjoyed by those inside, and this is just what we did. The central theme to the Bugatti project is thus very simple and rational: the development of precise functions and practical elements that respond to the need of those working inside and provide greater satisfaction to the personnel at all levels".

Many of the objectives cited by Benedini have been reached. The majority of the visitors to the Campogalliano industrial complex are thoroughly impressed; not so much by the works' beauty or lack of it - aesthetics being a very subjective concept - as by the environment, the light, the cleanliness, and above all by the motivation of the personnel. The place really does not have the air of an

The simple, linear architecture of the Ora Styling Centre expresses the criteria of rationality and functionality that permeate the entire project. In the photo above, the clean, modern facade. Right, a close up of the entrance portal which resembles the drawbridge of an ancient castle.

engineering establishment, but seems much more akin to something completely different, a hotel perhaps, or a clinic or residential centre. This is also one of the true strengths of the new Bugatti architecture: social improvement and new substance to the concept of the "machine civilization".

Turning now to the Styling Centre at Ora, whilst the style is different, as is the function of the building, the general design philosophy has the same intellectual basis. As Signora Renata Kettmeir Artioli says, "We have whole-heartedly adopted the concept followed by Ettore Bugatti of providing relaxing environments in which people feel good. When you come down to it, we spend most of our lives working, why then work in bunkers without light, without windows and with no direct or indirect contact with the outside world?"

"When we decided to establish the Bugatti Cultural Centre at Ora which was to collect, conserve and protect all the wonderful creations of the Bugatti family it was clear that we would have to find a setting in keeping with both the historical-artistic value of the objects and the basic philosophy of their creators. This complex was not intended as a static museum

→

dedicated to the Bugatti dynasty and its creations, but as a dynamic centre destined to disseminate knowledge of the family's cultural and artistic values and to further develop its ideas and projects". These basic programmes and ideas were well assimilated by Ambrosini, the Bolzano architect, who successfully developed the innovative concepts inherent to the project. The disposition of the volumes of the Ora complex was established in relation to the need to transform the building's ground floor into a large, luminous meeting place. It is something that you immediately notice as you cross the threshold of the entrance - an entrance resembling the drawbridge of an ancient castle, moat included, which creates an extraordinary optical and acoustic effect with the sound of running water and the red reflections of the portal. "This large central zone", continues Signora Artioli, "is the heart of the complex, the very hub of the company. It is a very flexible area which can be used to hold exhibitions, meetings, conferences and even concerts. The layout of the whole complex had precise objectives in

Above, the large, luminous hall is the hub around which the Ora Styling Centre's activities revolve. It is a very flexible area used for exhibitions, meetings and cultural events of various kinds. Above, right, the characteristic glazing of the entrance.

terms of communications, to create a dialogue with the outside world, to present the cars, the objects in the Bugatti collection, the family history and the documents contained in the archives as well as possible".

The Bugatti world at Ora gravitates around this luminous hall-garden with its many plants and flower beds. The pilot shop with its showroom, the archive, the graphics centre and other operational sectors are located in lateral wings and carry out their own specific functions. On the upper floor of the right-hand wing are the management and administrative offices, the commercial sector and the legal and buying departments. The left-hand wing houses the product side of the firm with the design, publicity and communications and accounts departments. As with the Campogalliano works the interior furnishings were chosen in the final design phase so as to be perfectly in keeping with the style of the building, the finishing materials adopted, and the specific function they were required to perform. "Certain elements are mass produced", concludes Signora Artioli, "but adapted to specific needs, others have been purpose designed and manufactured. It seemed to me to be a nice idea, as well as logical, to revive this typically Bugatti tradition as the furnishings are an important part of an integrated project".

Among the elements linking the Ora and Campogalliano complexes are the colour schemes, some of which are of course derived from the history and symbolism of the marque. The unmistakable blue of the racing cars for example, or the red of the background to the Bugatti badge. Strong colours of great visual impact which have been combined with, especially for the interiors, light, elegant, almost neutral colours which reinforce the sense of cleanliness and order generated by the buildings. The designers have also tried to approach, through the choice of colours or finishing materials, something existing in nature. Thus it is easy to find floors and walls in white marble with warm beige veining in the interiors of the new Bugatti architecture, whilst on the outside you find immaculate lawns or unusual paths paved with porphyry. Disseminated throughout the Ora and Campogalliano complexes as architectural and not simply decorative elements you find huge photographic reproductions of the cars of the past and present, or technical drawings of the most significant details underlining once again the stylistic continuity pervading Bugatti culture.

Technical dossier

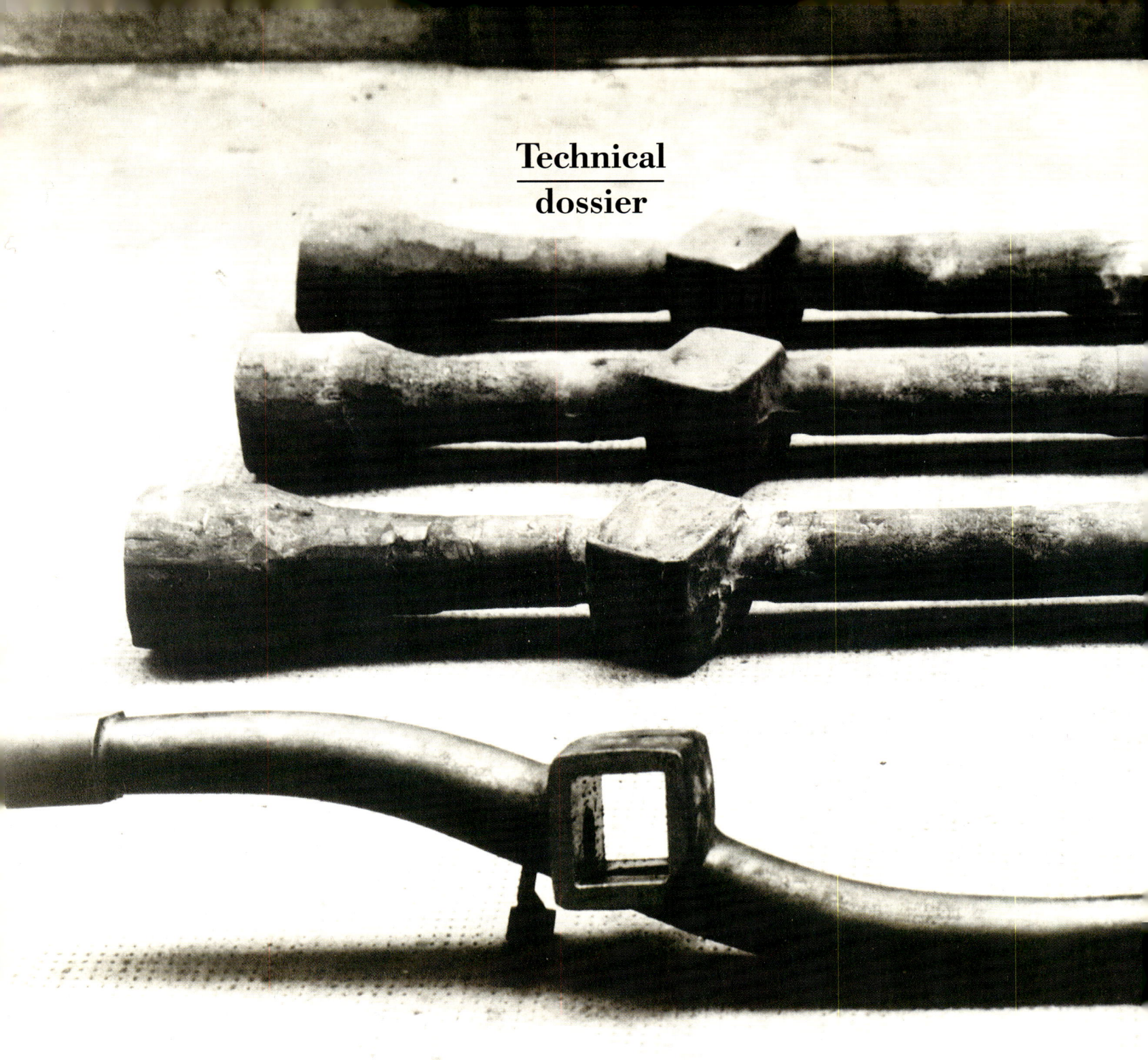

CHASSIS AND SUSPENSION: BUGATTI INNOVATION AND CONTINUITY

Bugatti chassis and suspension technology has always been in the avant-garde, ever since the granting of a celebrated patent in 1911. Today's EB 110 features a sophisticated fully independent twin wishbone suspension system. Testing plays a fundamental role in the development of the car. A new generation of Michelin tyres improves roadholding.

BY ENRICO BENZING

Top, an evocative period shot of the legendary front axle of the Type 35, a tangible symbol of the technically advanced engineering that could be carried out in the Molsheim workshops. This component is considered an authentic masterpiece of the forgeman's art.

It is impossible to establish valid links between the advanced and visionary engineering practised by Ettore Bugatti and modern design in the field of suspension or chassis in general. In the case of engines or transmissions, things are rather different: the Molsheim genius came up with multi-valve cylinder heads and four-wheel drive almost half a century ahead of their time. With the mechanical components there are authentic links between the various eras as there has been simple, constant and intense linear evolution. In contrast, at a certain point which we can date to around the end of the fifties, suspension design and the criteria relating to chassis construction were subjected to a clean break with the past and thus a bona fide revolution. The layouts featured on the EB 110, symbol of the Bugatti renaissance, are in many respects very similar to those developed for current Formula 1 cars (more sophisticated in certain cases) and represent a new and original technological field.

But if we take the time to consider how the great Bugatti understood engineering and automotive research, or to rummage through his countless patents, something of great significance comes to light: an awareness of and dedication to the same questions of chassis design with which we are dealing today in the realms of both competition machines and road-going supercars. The difference lies in the fact

Technical dossier

that today's designers are aware of the role played by suspension in automotive engineering progress, and are aware of just how much further progress there is to be made through the evolution of other elements - tyres for example - and new developments. Designers of the classic Bugatti era, on the other hand, ignored this aspect due the existence of insurmountable limits and because only power unit modifications guaranteed regular improvements in performance. The very fact that Bugatti was a guiding light in the history of automotive technology is reason enough to consider him an exception to every rule. At a time when all other designers were using leaf spring suspension he created, with the famous 1911 patent, the reversed rear leaf spring or quarter-elliptic spring, which for around 35 years was one of the secrets of his cars' superior roadholding. This meant that as well as having the spring under tension during the traction phase, the axle behaved correctly during rebound whilst the layout provided excellent longitudinal control. After all, looking at it with a modern eye, the relatively short quarter elliptic leaf spring acts as reaction strut does it not? If this is the case we are dealing with remarkable intuitions, combined with other inventions of note such as the hollow axle machined from a solid billet, usually steel but occasionally aluminium, and the cast aluminium alloy multi-piece wheels (reducing unsprung weight) introduced for the first time in the memorable French Grand Prix at Lyon in 1924. The latter were denied an immediate impact only through the disastrous performance of the new tyres, but were to become one of Molsheim's trademark features.

To get a better idea of Le Patron's dedication to the question of suspension design we have to go right back to the

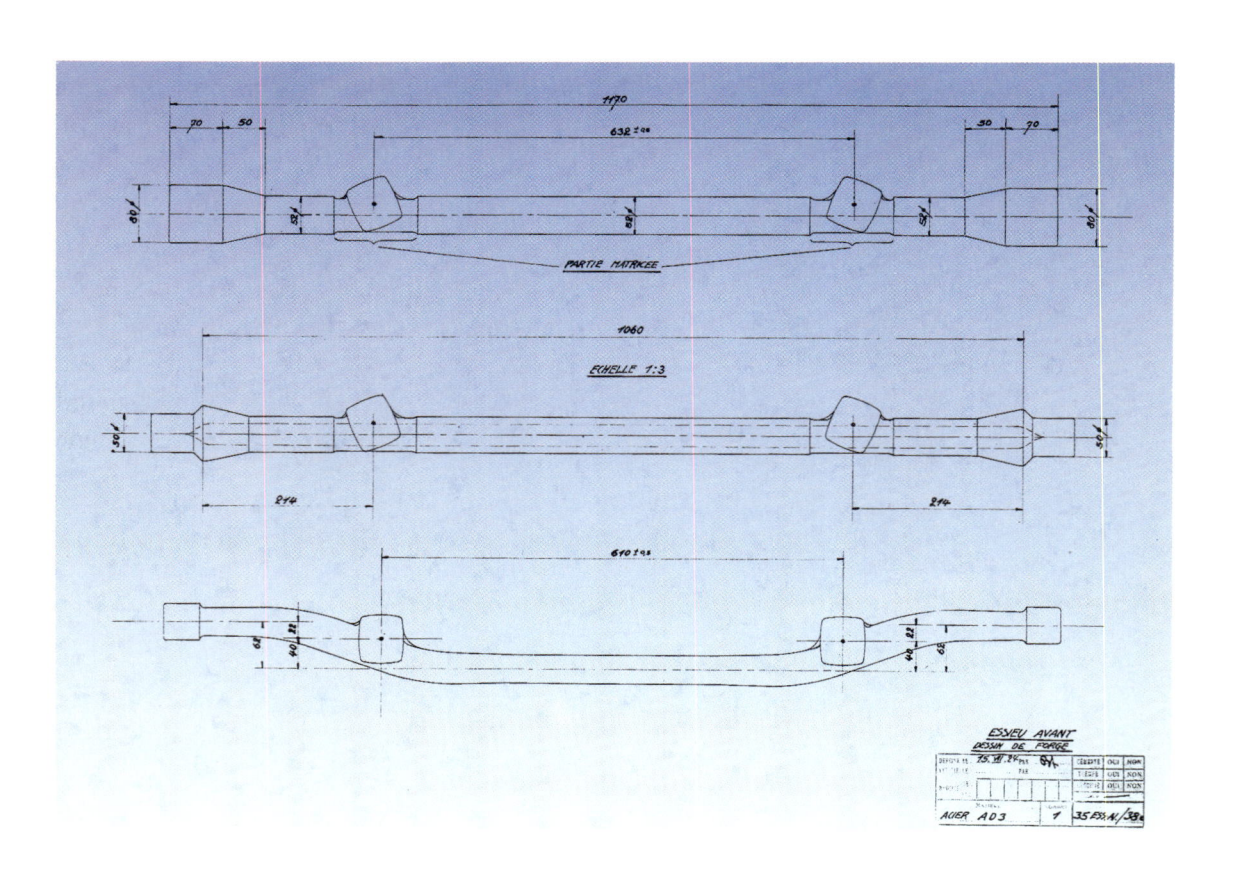

On the left, the original drawings of the Type 35 Grand Prix racer's hollowed axle. As can be seen in the photo above, the machined component was perfectly cylindrical on the outside and hollow inside, with solid ends allowing the secure mounting of the stub axle carriers.

In the drawings below, on the left the front suspension of the EB 110 with the double wishbones, and on the right the rear units with the two raised coil-over dampers pivoting on the upper wishbone. Bottom, see-through rendering of the car showing the suspension kinematics.

celebrated 1911 patent which demonstrates that he was already exploring the field of kinematics in full cognition of the facts. The first description of the invention even took into consideration lateral forces with the quarter-elliptic leaf spring flexibly attached to the chassis. As the patent says: "This is obtained by connecting the spring to the chassis through laterally sprung couplings". The spring-reaction arm allowed complex movements: one of the leaves could be fixed whilst the others twisted about the vertical axis. As was specified in the patent: "With this form of execution the raising and lowering of the car does not result in it being shifted from its longitudinal axis".

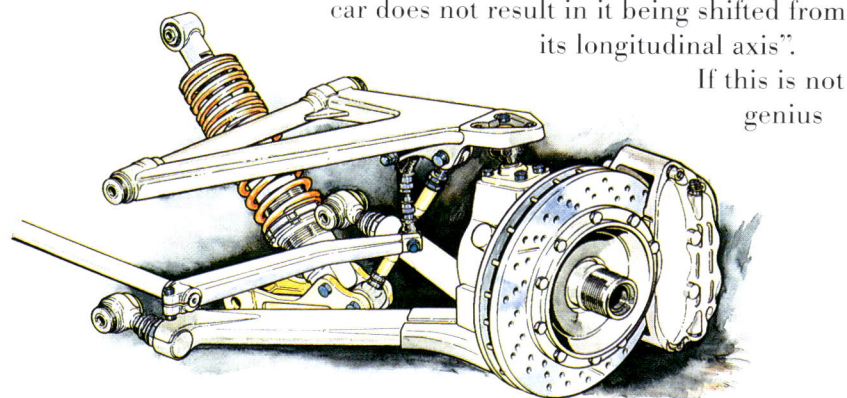

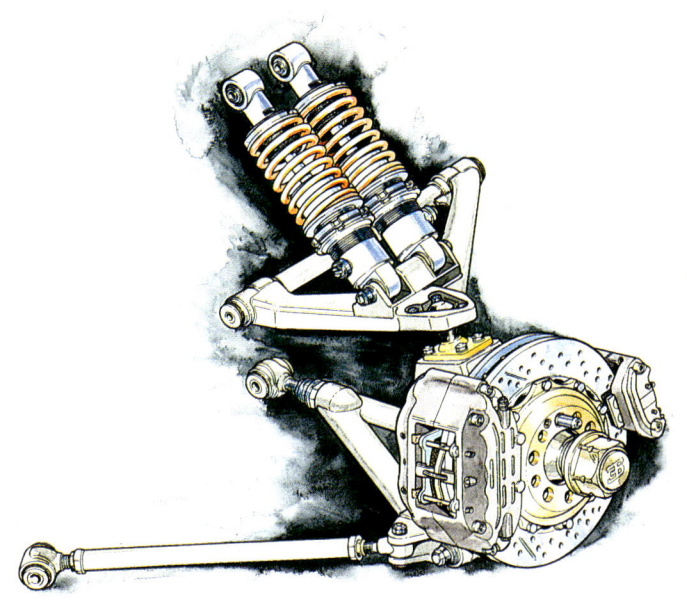

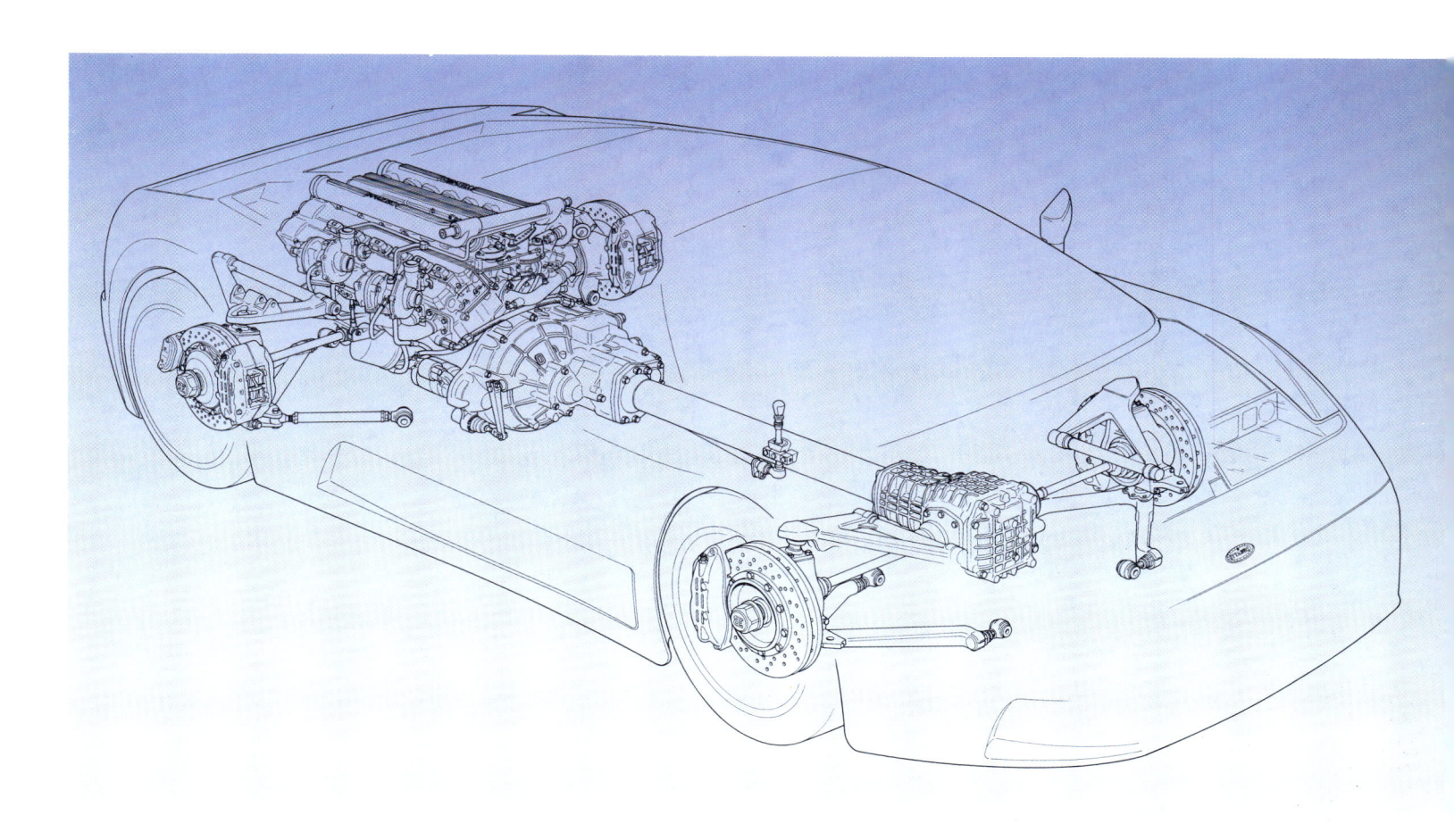

If this is not genius or the partial anticipation of concepts (and solutions) which have since become fundamental, then we may as well stop talking about the Bugatti legend. Examining the suspension layout of the EB 110 (the original model has already been joined by the "S" version and the four-door EB 112) we are struck by the radical developments that have been made in the area since the revolution mentioned above. These are based on the principle of fully independent double wishbone systems, with kinematic similarities between the front and rear axles in mid-engined cars.

The current Bugatti, for example, features a pull-rod system in the front double wishbone suspension, with a more conventional layout at the rear where the lower wishbone assumes a trapezoidal form through the addition of a strut (together with the inclination of the plane, this generates a self-steering effect in the rebound phase and the recovery of correct convergence). The rear layout also features original, high mounted, twin coil-over damper units pivoting on the upper wishbone.

A great advantage of fully independent suspension, leaving aside purely geometric aspects, is that it is possible to alter the parameters very easily when tuning the suspension to obtain the best compromise between often contrasting demands. Clearly, the choice of the pull-rod front system was dictated by the need to obtain valuable progressive springing and damping. In fact, the conventional actuation of the spring-damper unit offers the possibility of progressive rate springing, but the behaviour of the damper is unaltered. If on the other hand, as occurs with the pull-rod system, the progressiveness of the kinematics is precisely tuned the damper is also actively involved. Furthermore, unsprung weight is reduced with the pull-rod system, whilst the physical layout of the suspension elements facilitates the passage of the half-shafts. The same goes for the raised rear coil-over units; we should not forget that the Bugatti EB 110 is the world's only four-wheel drive supercar.

In the two photos above, the suspension layouts of the EB 110 seen from below, on the left, the rear unit with the lower wishbone in the foreground, on the right the twin wishbone front layout characterised by a pull-rod system. In the drawing below, the rational arrangement of the mechanical and suspension components.

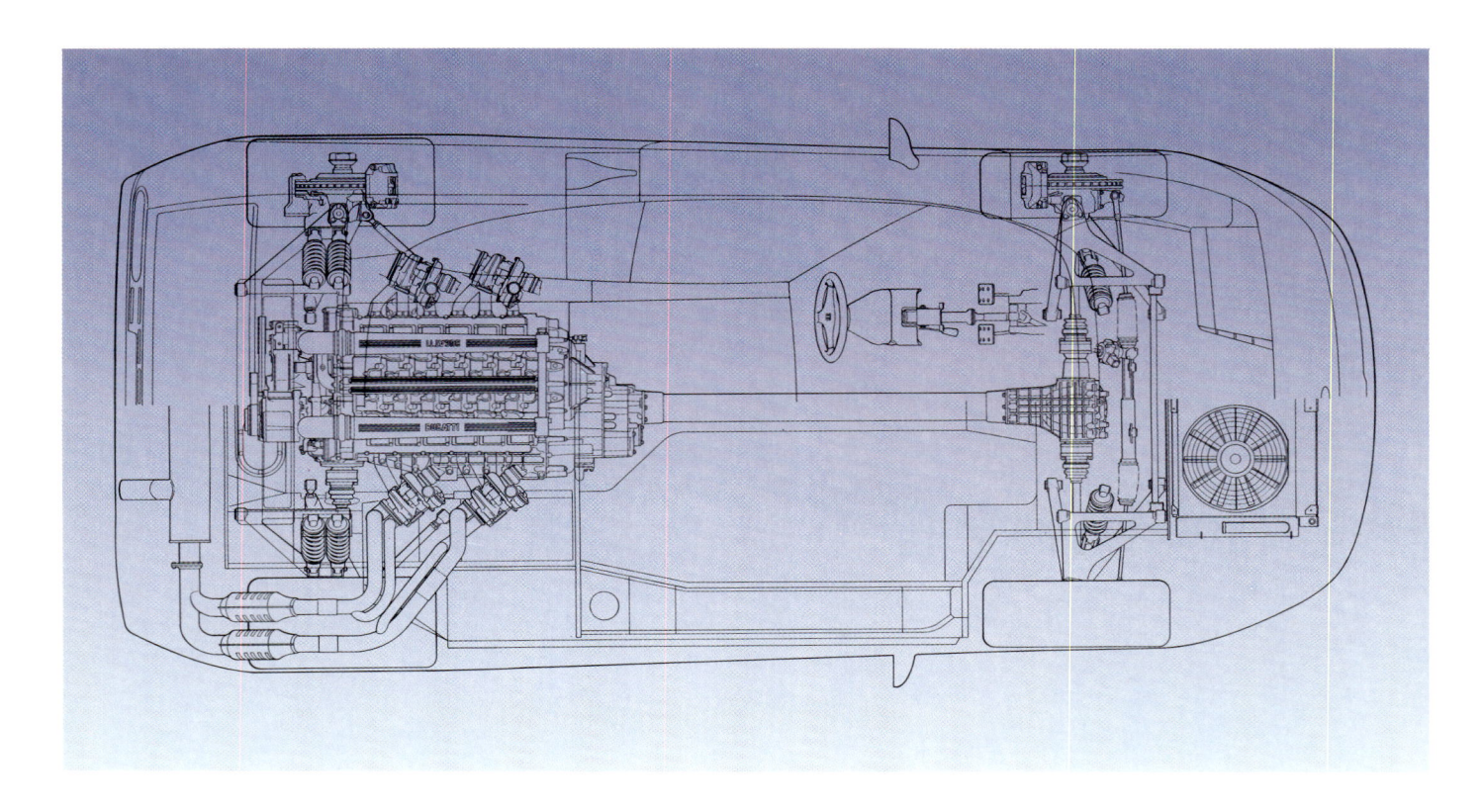

In the photo above, a detail of the one-piece hollow front axle of the Type 35. The accuracy and high level of finish of the Bugatti workmanship is in clear evidence. In order to achieve this result the axle started out as a solid billet which was hollowed out and then shaped.

Given the car's remarkable compactness the layout of the rear suspension had to allow for strictly limited space, both vertically due to the coachwork design, and width-wise thanks to the V-12 engine with its lateral exhausts and the gearbox parallel to the block.

The division of the loading with the two coil-over dampers allows the same size units to be used as at the front, with only the ratings being altered. However, with the specific problems of sporting use in mind, a single large spring and damper have been employed on the "S" version. Designers are blessed with often surprising resourcefulness and in the end the space for the larger units was found. In any case, however exacting the design and engineering process behind the development of the suspension of an ultra-sporting car, it pales into relative insignificance alongside the programme of testing, development, fine tuning and continual research that follows.

The comprehensive notes compiled by Bugatti's specialist four-wheel drive and high performance car dynamics clearly illustrate how the EB 110 was subjected to a painstaking development process before achieving the degrees of stability and manoeuvrability that have made it a class leader.

The first step concerned the choice of tyres, an enormously difficult decision given the car's astonishing performance capabilities. Roadholding depends entirely on the tyre to tarmac contact between the car and road. The EB 110 project began with 17" rims fitted with tyres with too small a section and with a slight difference between the front and rear covers: 225 against 245 mm section width. The earliest tests proved that this type of tyre could not provide the optimum results required. 18" rims were thus adopted, and with our help Michelin - Bugatti is fortunate in that it can rely on the collaboration of such a technically advanced marque - developed a new generation of tyres which are still exclusive to Bugatti. Section dimensions are now 245/40 at the front and 325/30 at the rear with, it hardly needs to be said, construction and compound characteristics that guarantee optimum balance between the front and rear axles. We have not ignored the principle whereby a 4x4 car should present the same rolling circumference on both sets of tyres, but in this case the use of identical tyres is impossible given the car's weight distribution and given the demands of the longitudinal and lateral forces acting on the front and rear axles.

The research thus had to concentrate on special cornering force characteristics under the effect of lateral and propulsive forces - forces that are far removed from the norms with all-wheel drive. Only at a later stage did research into the kinematics begin with a theoretical base and exhaustive testing, often with diverse compromises being tried in the search for the optimum balance between traction and stability.

Thus it was - although these explanations offer but a vague idea of the significance of the technological applications involved - that the EB 110 became a paragon of stability and driveability with the intrinsic performance potential we are all familiar with. If the EB 110's manoeuvrability matches that of the best compact saloon, if its roadholding is such as to transform roads into rails and if its driver does never even notices the four-wheel drive, it is all down to superlative technology of the kind demanded by Ettore Bugatti.

Special
Japan

PAST, PRESENT AND FUTURE IN THE REALM OF THE SAMURAI

An agreement has signed by Bugatti Automobili and Nicole Racing Japan which becomes the sole distributor of Campogalliano's super-cars in the Land of the Rising Sun. The passion for historic Bugattis continues to grow, as two million Japanese were able to see for themselves the world's most up-to-date and fastest Grand Turismo car at the Tokyo Motor Show.

BY NORIKO WELPONER

Since the founding of the new Bugatti companies, Ettore Bugatti's birthday on September 15th has been marked by a series of special events. In 1993, the 112th anniversary of Ettore's birth, one of these events was the signing of a contract between Bugatti Automobili SpA and Nicole Racing Japan Co. Ltd., which was appointed sole distributor for Japan within the framework of the policy of global extension of the Bugatti cars distribution network. The Bugatti models currently imported onto the Japanese market are the Grand Turismo EB 110 and the EB 110 Supersport. Importation of the EB 112 Sports Saloon is also planned as soon as it goes into production.

Nicole Racing Japan held a press conference, at which Romano Artioli was present, to announce their appointment. A large number of motoring journalists from the motoring sector attended, including several reporters from important dailies who devoted a fair amount of space to the presentation.

The press conference was opened with a speech by Mr Iwaki, our representative in Tokyo, introducing the new distributor, Mr Nico Röhreke, who has many years experience on the Japanese market. Mr Röhreke came to Japan 24 years ago with his father, at that time attached to the German embassy, and from 1974 to 1982 he was an active racing driver. He now speaks better Japanese than the Japanese themselves; it was in this language that he expressed his enthusiasm for the new Bugatti cars.

Considering the great prestige of the Bugatti marque, the contract with Nicole Racing Japan is of particular importance and concerns both marketing and special technical assistance for the whole Japanese territory. This well-known and respected company has been handling prestige European cars in Japan for more than 15 years, with a degree of success and dynamism particularly evident in the availability of BMW cars and the special

In the photo on the left, Nico Röhreke, Chairman of Nicole Racing Japan, sole distributor of Bugatti cars on the Japanese market.

On the right, the elegant entrance to the Nicole Racing Japan Co. premises at Kawasaki. Below, Romano Artioli, President of Bugatti Automobili, and Nico Röhreke, President of Nicole Racing Japan announcing the details of the new agreement to the Japanese press.

Alpina models. The future plans of Nicole Racing Japan include active collaboration with Bugatti Japan Co. Ltd, importer of the Bugatti cars, both in type approval work and in promoting special activities for customers. Mr Röhreke inaugurated his distributorship on 11 November by inviting his customers for a cocktail, to look round his showrooms and offices and to inspect the Bugatti cars. Guests included Mr Yoshiho Matsuda, famous collector and owner of four motor museums and three museums of art; Mr Shotaro Kobayashi, member of the Bugatti committee of honour, vintage Bugatti owner and founder of the Car Graphic Group, accompanied by his wife, Mrs Mariko Kobayashi; and Mr Sokichi Shikiba, opinion leader, ex-racing driver, winner of the first Japanese Grand Prix and owner of the first Bugatti EB 110 Supersport.

As the date of the Tokyo Motor Show approached following Mr Röhreke's appointment, he made a last minute application for space to set up a Bugatti stand, which was of course received long after the official closing date. His request was enthusiastically received by the organisers, and the number of people flocking to the Bugatti stand once again demonstrated the degree of interest generated by this marque, to the extent that the Bugattis were the stars of the show. Given that Tokyo is considered the most striking and most visited Motor Show in the world, this was no mean achievement.

The Tokyo Motor Show, which is held every two years, is recognised as one of the three most important motor shows in the world, along with Detroit and Frankfurt. For this the 30th edition, the theme was "Ecolution" (ecology and evolution) in car innovation. The total number of automobile manufacturers present this year was 352, on a newly built site covering an area of 47,468 square metres in Makuhari. The record daily attendance was 205,700 visitors, and the total for the whole period, from 23 October to 7 November was 1,810,000.

The Japanese national television network NHK dedicated a two-hour programme to the Tokyo Motor Show, focusing on 10 selected cars. Among them was of course the Bugatti. It was presented as the ultimate aspiration for the committed enthusiast. And in fact one of the programme's presenters, Mr Yosuke Natsuki, concluded by saying "If I were to choose one [of these cars] for myself, it would be the Bugatti!"

Special Japan

The origins and history of the Classic Car Club, a group of true enthusiasts who, since 1956, have succeeded in collecting and restoring some of the most exclusive cars in Japan.

BY SHOTARO KOBAYASHI

The Classic Car Club of Japan (CCCJ) was founded in 1956 by a small group of people based in Tokyo. The linchpin of the group was the late Mr Tokutaro Hama.

He was recognised as a pioneer of the vintage car movement in Japan at a time when old cars were, like shabby old clothes, regarded with derision and pity rather than respect.

Mr Hama, a professor of art, already owned a small vintage collection which included a Bugatti Type 35C imported by a Portuguese diplomat in the 1930's, a FWD Alvis and an Hispano-Suiza H6B among others.

It was only natural that he should become the first President of the CCCJ. Some thirty-five years later, in 1990, I was elected the fourth President.

In retrospect, 1950-55 was a critical period as far as the old car movement in Japan was concerned.

This was because the pre-war survivors, the real cars in our eyes, which had still been providing yeoman's service in austere post-war Japan, were quickly disappearing from the scene, replaced by "modern" tin boxes such as the locally assembled Austin A40/A50 and the Hillman Minx, or the precious few post-war imports.

I well remember how Mr Hama used to say "Quick boys! Let's buy them now. We can always rebuild them later".

The members of the CCCJ, mostly young and impecunious enthusiasts like myself, thus launched their laudable campaign to save precious old cars from the scrap-heaps. We were a very small group and funds were, as now, strictly limited, but we are proud that the cars we managed to save included three Rolls-Royce Phantoms, the remains of a Hispano-Suiza H6B, a very nice 8th Series Lancia Lambda, two big Alvises, an MG K3 Magnette (one of the two prototypes) and a Type 23 Brescia Bugatti.

All of these cars were later rebuilt and

Top left, the President of the Classic Car Club Japan, Shotaro Kobayashi at the wheel of his Brescia Bugatti. The other photos show aspects of the club's activities.

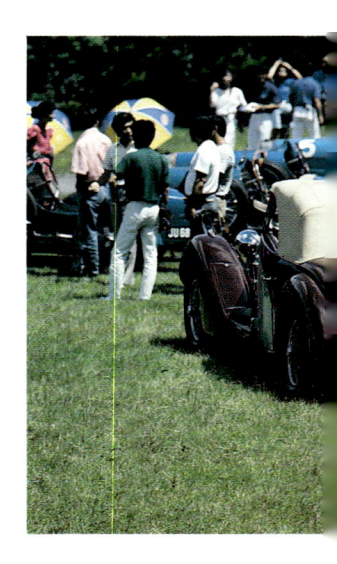

was formed within the CCCJ. According to our research forty-six Bugattis now definitely reside in this country as follows: Type 17 (one), Type 13 16-valve (six), Type 22 (two), Type 23 (two), Type 35T (one), Type 35C (two), Type 35B (five), Type 37 (two), Type 37A (three), Type 40 (three), Type 41 (one, ex-Cunningham Kellner Coupé), Type 43 (two), Type 44 (three), Type 46 (one), Type 51 (one), Type 55 (one), Type 57 (four), Type 57C (four), Type 73C (one). It is a great pity that due to bad traffic conditions here, it has become increasingly difficult, if not entirely impossible, to organise any open road event.

So much so that our activities tend to be limited to speed events on circuits or social occasions on private land. The annual Bugatti Day is a good example of the latter and some twenty examples of the marque usually take part. On the other hand, there are two speed events a year at the Tsukuba Circuit near Tokyo and a few GP models usually compete against Alfas, Rileys, MG's and sundry Austin Seven derivations.

However, some of the Japanese Bugatti drivers prefer competing in overseas events. Back in 1979 a CCCJ contingent of eight cars and drivers went to Macau and took part in a vintage car race held in conjunction with the Macau GP. Among them were a Type 13 and a Type 37 which finished 3rd and 6th.

In 1985 my wife and I competed in the Monte Carlo Rally with Uwe Hucke's Type 51, and then in 1989 I successfully completed the Mille Miglia with a Type 43 Grand Sport.

So you see, although we drive on the "wrong" side of the road and speak differently, what we do with our beloved Bugattis is more or less the same as that practised by enthusiasts all over the world.

some of them are kept in active use today. Incidentally, the Brescia is mine. I discovered it in 1955 in Osaka, took ten years to persuade its owner to part with it, and another twelve to restore it. It took so long because firstly it was in such a horrible state, and secondly because I did all the mechanical work myself, mostly at weekends and late at night after work, and not without a foolish mistake or two.

In the early 70's when the Japanese economy started booming and strict control of foreign currencies was finally relaxed, a gold rush of historic car imports arrived here all of a sudden, perhaps to the chagrin of some overseas enthusiasts.

The population of Bugattis in Japan thus escalated and it now seems to have reached some fifty cars.

Luckily most of them belong to good homes rather than to speculators or over-night collectors.

In 1991 the Japanese Bugatti Register

Special Japan

The city of Kobe hosted the successful and evocative exhibition dedicated to the birth and development of the Bugatti legend.

BY IVO CECI

At Fashion Town, in a twenty-first century cityscape of white skyscrapers and enchanting gardens, on an artificial island reached from the of Kobe (Japan's most important port) via a driver-less monorail controlled by an invisible, infallible computer, it came as something of a surprise to see ranks of waving flags bearing the familiar red oval. They lead to the starting point of journey through time that covered one hundred and ten years, an evocative historical and social carousel contained in the exclusive exhibition "The Bugatti Legend", held from 1 July to 12 September, 1993. In the half-light visitors were confronted with images formed from real objects set against fantastic backdrops. Clever lighting and an appropriate soundtrack created a magical atmosphere which helped the public lose themselves in what they were seeing. The first section concerned the world of Carlo and Rembrandt Bugatti illustrated with their works of art, and led into the section dealing with the infancy of the Bugatti legend: the young Ettore, his first tricycle, his first inventions and his first successes.

The narrative then moved on to the birth of the Molsheim factory and its

Above, a panel from the exhibition "The Bugatti Legend" dedicated to the "boundless horizons" of thr great marque. Bugatti designed and produced avant-grade planes, high-speed trains, ship, motorboats and bicycles.

Below, the backdrop of the section presenting emergenle of Ettori Bugatti's genius and his first technical successes. All this panels, illustrating the evocative Japanese Exhibition, were produced by Studio Salvadori to designs by Chiara Boeri.

enchanted atmosphere: the twenties. the first fantastic touring and competition cars. The hundreds of victories, from the Targa Florio at Brescia to the Le Mans 24 Hours, by way of the Monte Carlo Grand Prix, with legendary cars such as the Type 35, the "Tank", the Type 13, the Type 51, the "Cigare" and the Type 59.

But in those years Bugatti was not only synonymous with competition cars, there were also other machines capable of providing their fortunate owners with unique sensations: the Type 43, the Type 55, the fabulous Royale.

Jean Bugatti then entered the equation with his sinuous, almost sensual lines, and his masterful colour combinations which added dynamism, lightness and elegance to the masterpieces produced at Molsheim and became a new point of reference for coachwork styling. Completing this world were planes, trains and boats: testimony to the eclectic genius of the Bugattis.

Up until this point the story had been continuous, beginning in turn of the century Milan and reaching France in the 30's, on the eve of tragedy.

At this point of the exhibition, having turned a corner, the visitors were confronted with a bright, blue and aggressive present in the form of a splendid EB 110 set against an immense red oval. The journey into legend then came to an end, and the visitors once again found themselves in the landscape of modern Japan, a country which more than any other is focused on the future, but one which manages to maintain its ancient traditions. The people of the Land of the Rising Sun who flocked to the Kobe exhibition (over 60,000 enthusiasts) welcomed and appreciated this modern European legend with its mere hundred-year history with great enthusiasm and admiration.

News

POLLUTION? NO THANKS.

Bugatti Electronics' Greengas device makes a notable contribution to the reduction of both pollution and fuel consumption and opens up new horizons for the use of gaseous fuels (LPG or methane) in the place of petrol and diesel oil. The use of this new injection device allows exhaust emissions and fuel consumption to be drastically reduced whilst still maintaining, or even improving, the engine's original power output. The new gaseous fuel injection device's secret lies in the application of the principle whereby perfect consumption is a requisite of optimum emissions and fuel consumption figures. To achieve this state the mixing of the air and fuel needs to be properly governed, with constant monitoring of the ambient conditions and, in the case of LPG, of the continual variation in composition of the fuel. The Bugatti Greengas device analyses the combustion parameters in real time and instantaneously modifies the quantity of fuel to be injected into the combustion chamber to achieve greatest efficiency. In the case of a petrol powered vehicle converted to run on LPG or methane with the Bugatti Greengas device, there is no noticeable fall-off in power compared with the traditional fuel, whilst fuel consumption may be reduced by as much as 30%, especially when the engine is asked to produce maximum power. It should be emphasised that this is accompanied by a drastic reduction in toxic emissions throughout the rev range. The Bugatti Greengas system is based on an extremely sophisticated computer using minaturized technology, and a single extremely compact injector which can be fitted to the fuel system of any internal combustion engine. It is maintenance-free and needs no further tuning as it is self-adaptive and self-adjusting. The switch from the original fuel to the alternative, be it LPG or methane, and vice versa, takes place automatically without any noticeable change and without altering the running of the engine in any way. All system functions can be programmed via suitable software.

BUGATTI RALLY

The traditional International Bugatti Meeting will take place in Italy this year from 5 to 10 June.
Organized by the Bugatti Cultural Centre with the help of the Bugatti Club Italia, the event will offer "art, culture and emotions" to the participants.
Open to Bugattisti throughout the world, the meeting is undoubtedly the key event on the international Bugatti collectors' calendar.
Cars are expected to arrive from as far afield as the United States, Japan and Australia.
The International Meeting in Italy will visit the most beautiful areas of the provinces of Mantova, Modena, Padova, Rovigo, Treviso, Venezia and Verona.
An unforgettable rendezvous of all the cars in the elegant and exclusive setting of Piazza San Marco in Venice will take place during the event.

News

THE DESERT QUEEN

It might appear to be a photo-montage or a concept for a spectacular publicity campaign, but instead the fantastic EB 110 actually did become the Queen of the Arabian desert for a few days. Testing in extreme conditions forms part of a precise Bugatti research and development programme.

Ingegnere Pavel Rajmis left Campogalliano on 28 November with an EB 110 and three mechanics, Federico Canovi, Claudio Salardi and Andrea Stenico, and headed to Dubai in Saudi Arabia. Here they carried out a number of tests on the behaviour and performance of the car at temperatures of over 38°C coupled with high percentages of humidity.

The tests were carried out for over two weeks at speeds of up to 320 kph on the motorways, in town in the stop-go conditions of city traffic and finally on desert tracks to check the sand-proofing.
The EB 110, having passed these tests with flying colours, is now ready to take on even the desert challenge.

ADIEU "PRINCESS"

Unfortunately Elizabeth Junek is no longer among us.
The great Czech driver we nick-named "Princess" in the article dedicated to her in the fifth edition of our magazine has always been a point of reference for Bugatti. A living symbol of an unrepeatable period, the twenties, in which the image of the marque assumed a precise, indelible definition. The spirit of the Bugatti legend, its true essence, stems in part from the actions, the style and the passion of the personalities who acompanied Ettore in the realization of his dreams.
Part of this legend is undoubtedly linked to those thrilling years between 1925 and 1928 when, through her incredible sporting successes, the meteoric Elizabeth succeeded in eclipsing the achievements of the titans of the automotive world. She retired from racing in 1929, but her name has always remained an integral part of the Bugatti story.

International events

THE KLAUSEN'S SECOND COMING

A thrilling recreation of the legendary hillclimb held on the traditional course, the Klausenrennen Memorial 1993 attracted 166 motorcycles and 280 cars, all constructed before 1940. A remarkable squad of no less than 24 historic Bugattis took part in this incredible revival. The Swedish driver Per Larsson in a Type 35 C set the fastest time of the day in the Sport D2 category.

BY FRANCO ZAGARI

The success enjoyed by the Klausenrennen Memorial can hardly be put down to a stroke of luck which benefited a group of relatively inexperienced, makeshift organizers. Quite the contrary, it was the fruit of painstaking preparation that began in earnest a year and a half earlier, and of a singularly spectacular idea conceived even earlier, the feasibility of which had to be carefully analysed.

The preparation involved above all a diplomatic operation intent on sounding out and obtaining the interest and cooperation of the three local authorities directly concerned: Altdorf, birthplace of William Tell no less, Glarus and Linthal. The next hurdles to be overcome were the federal prohibitions regarding automotive competition. With this accomplished the organization of the event could get under way. This phase began in the second half of 1992, a good year before the Memorial was due to take place.

It should therefore come as no surprise to learn that Bernard Brägger and his colleagues enjoyed a triumphant success with the participation of four hundred and forty-six historic vehicles (166 motorcycles and 280 cars) all built before 1940.

Among the motorcycles, one of the most interesting examples - to tell the truth they

Original photos of Bugattis on the Klausenrennen taken from the archives of Franco Zagari. This page, right, Sojka, first in the 1500 class in 1934 with the Type 51 A. On the facing page, top, Achille Varzi controls the potent Type 53 in 1932; bottom, Gunther Burghaller, first in class in 1934, with the Type 35 B.

were all interesting in one way or another - was the 1892 Hildebrenad & Wolfmüller, the first serially produced machine and one featuring oil circulating through the frame tubes. Walking round the square in Glarus, the assembly and registration point, you could not help but drool over one vehicle after another, naturally pausing over those machines that you had never had the chance to see before. The Steyer types 100 and 120, a fabulous Hispano Suiza 116 and the Maybach SW38, but also the cyclecars or the little Rosengart LR2 or the Aero 662. The only →

This page, right, the determination of Mrs Kozmian taking her Type 37 A through a hairpin during the 1934 edition. Above, the pharmacist from Bern, Horning, racing in the same year with his Type 43. The course for this famous hillclimb remained unchanged for the ten editions held between 1922 and 1934 and was 21.5 kilometres long.

International events

problem was that a single day just was not enough to enjoy the spectacle to the full. Given the fame of the Klausenrennen, there could hardly have failed to be a substantial Bugatti contingent present at the start. In the past the cars from Molsheim had won the event outright on two occasions in 1929 and 1930 with Louis Chiron at the wheel of a Type 51 and a Type 45, as well as scoring numerous victories in the minor classes in the hands of privateers. The course used for the ten editions held between 1922 and 1934 was twenty-one kilometres and five hundred metres long, with two steep and demanding corkscrew climbs split by a gentleslope of about seven kilometres on which used to be established a timing station. It is virtually unchanged today except for the asphalting of the once unmetalled road surface.

No less than twenty-four Bugattis, covering virtually the entire range of the marque's competition cars along with a number of magnificent GT's, took part in the event, headed by two Type 13 Brescias. The Swedish driver Per Larsson with a Type 35 C obtained the fastest time of the day in the Sport D2 category: 24' 02.68", climbing at an average speed of 53.650 kph, whilst the German Walter Rothlauf, driving a Type 37 A took the honours in category B with a time of 19' 12.26". The other German driver Joseph Kleine, went just as well in class 3,000 with a Type 35 B taking 20' 14.71" to complete the climb. The most interesting "blue" notes were, given their fascinating technical specifications, inevitably provided by the Type 45 sixteen-cylinder machine driven by the Englishman John Howell, and the four-wheel drive Type 53 ably guided

In the photo above, the great Louis Chiron, dominator of the Klausenrennen in 1930, with the 16-cylinder Bugatti Type 45. The Monaco-born driver is portrayed at the beginning of the special timed seven-kilometre gently sloping section which separated the two steep and demanding series of climbing hairpins which were such a feature of the course. The greatest drivers of the twenties and thirties met at the Klausen.

Alfa Romeo was also very well represented but strangely, as was the case with the Bugattis, there were no Italian entries among them. The only Italians taking part were Silvio Ubertino and Erwin Botzner with two admirable Gilera 500's.
What was particularly striking about the event, apart from the commendable organisation worthy of the Swiss reputation for precision, was the demonstration of just how deeply rooted are the memories of Tazio Nuvolari with graffiti in his honour emblazoned on the rocks at both series of hairpins.

Numerous historic Bugattis captured the interest of the enthusiasts at the Klausenrennen Memorial 1993. On the right, the passage of two Bugattisti at the exit of a hairpin bend. Above, the Type 35 driven by Roger Berthélèmy at speed. Below, the cars taking part mustered for registration in the square at Glarus.

round the hairpins by the Frenchman Henry Roseau. The wonderful weather enjoyed on the eve of the event had turned to thundery showers by race day. This did not deter either the numerous spectators or the competitors, and the full programme was completed. The spectators encouraged each competitor with enthusiastic applause, and were often surprised at the speeds of some of the older vehicles and captivated by the smell of hot oil and the full-blooded roar of the engines. The Mercedes-Benz drivers were warmly received, and as well as the private entries the factory had sent along some exceptional machinery from its museum such as the 1908 Benz G.P., the 600-hp W125 and the W154 from 1939.

International events

Top, left, the elegant and shapely Type 57 of Leonhart Helmreich. Above, Hans Ruedi Schmid shows off his splendid Type 57 cabriolet. Far left, the unmistakeable shape of René Rieger's Type 37 A. Left, period costume was also a part of the Klausenrennen Memorial scene.

The Bugattis present at the Klausenrennen Memorial 1993

Number	Driver	Model	Nationality
47	Walter Grell	T44	CH
72	Hans Ruedi Schmid	T57	CH
186	Hubert Strohammer	T49	D
45	Per Larsson	T35C	S
211	Heinz Wiemeier	T30	D
208	Alex Füllermann	T13B	CH
242	Heiner Lohrer	T37A	D
240	René Rieger	T37A	F
243	P. Douchet de Rovére	T39	F
241	Walter Rothlauf	T37A	D
239	Martin Strohhammer	T13B	D
245	Hans Matti	T35C	CH
246	Roger Berthélèmy	T35	F
248	Martin Pfrunder	T35B	CH
247	Marc Blanc	T35	F
249	F. Joseph Kleine	T35B	D
257	Leonhard Helmreich	T57	D
315	L. Michel Quaterlat	49/57	F
324	Charles Renaud	T51	CH
442	Henry Roseau	T53	F
391	Bart Rosman	T37	NL
393	Ivan Dutton	T35	GB
398	John Howell	T45	GB
437	Lord Fitlroy	T51	GB

Near right, the Type 35 C of Per Larsson and, centre, the Type 35 of Marc Blanc in its characteristic amaranth livery. Below, the little Type 13 B of Martin Strohammer. Far right, top, the turtle symbol of Tazio Nuvolari painted on the rocks, centre, the four-wheel drive Type 53 driven by Henry Roseau, bottom, the black Type 39 of Douchet de Rovére.

The Klausenrennen meetings

Year	Winner	Car	Time
1922	M. Nieth	Hispano Suiza	21'43"0
1923	H. Rutzler	Steyr	20'24"4
1924	O. Merz	Mercedes	18'48"6
1925	G. Masetti	Sunbeam	17'28"8
1926	Kessler	Alfa P2	18'42"8
1927	Rosenberger	Mercedes GP/914	17'17"0
1929	L. Chiron	Bugatti T51	16'42"4
1930	L. Chiron	Bugatti T45	16'24"8
1932	Caracciola	Alfa P3	15'50"0
1934	Caracciola	Mercedes Benz W25	15'22"2

Sport story

A TRUE GENTLEMAN DRIVER

René Dreyfus as remembered by his friend the American World Champion Phil Hill. In the twenties and thirties Dreyfus, born in Nice, succeeded in defeating the legendary figures of the sport on numerous occasions. A symbolic figure in the history of motor sport, he made a name for himself early on in his career at the wheel of the Molsheim thoroughbreds.

BY PHIL HILL

It has become almost difficult to think of René Dreyfus as a racing driver. In this era of overpaid, spoiled sporting heroes, how could this quiet, quiet impeccably dressed, definition of a gentleman have been a heroic racing driver? And yet René Dreyfus competed against and beat the legends of the sport at a time when driving a racing car was a very hazardous profession. What's more, he did it with style, finesse and precision. Look through the photos of René driving and try to find one in which he is fighting a car, manhandling it through a tight turn or high-speed curve. I've never seen one. Yet he was so quick and he consistently finished at the top.
Born in Nice in 1905, René's first race was at the wheel of the family Mathis on June 13, 1924, with his brother and life-long friend Maurice in the seat next to him. Their mother wasn't too happy about this outing, but was none the lass convinced that René should continue to race and that the family needed a Brescia Bugatti, which promptly became his second racing car.
Next came a Bugatti Type 37A.
The area around Nice and the south of France was a hot bed of racing activity, and René's career followed that of another Riviera resident, Louis Chiron, and the pair soon became friends. Both drivers made names for themselves on the Riviera and then expanded their horizons.
By 1928 René was ready to try his first major event, the Targa Florio, in which he finished eighth in the 37A.
The following year René received an invitation to drive in the inaugural Monaco GP, where he finished fifth overall and first in the 1500 cc class. When the Monaco-winning Bugatti Type 35B of "Williams" was put up for sale a well-to-do Parisian bought it and let René race it... and his career was launched.

On the facing page, a tribute by the painter Jorge Ferreyra-Basso to René Dreyfus, portrayed at the wheel of his Bugatti Type 37A, the car which he drove in 1928. Above, a snapshot from 3 April, 1932, taken before the start of the Grand Prix of Tunisia. From the left are Ruggeri, Fagioli, Ernesto Maserati and Dreyfus. Right, a portrait of the Nice-born champion.

Within a year René confirmed his promise by winning the 1930 Monaco Grand Prix in an upset.
That same year he won the Grand Prix de la Marne at Reims, and thought it might lead to a factory drive with Bugatti. Ettore Bugatti wasn't interested, and even snubbed the young driver, but the Maserati brothers invited him to join their team, throwing in the French Maserati distributorship on the side. René drove for the Maseratis throughout 1931 with little success, and began the 1932 season before problems between driver and team caused them to separate early in the season.
René then raced a Bugatti owned by his friend Chiron for the remainder of the season, a successful period marred by the most serious crash of his career.
René's wishes were fulfilled the following year when he signed on with Bugatti for what would be a two-season stint racing Le Patron's cars and living at Molsheim. During this period, René drove the Types 51, 54, and 59, and set the course record at the La Turbie hillclimb in the difficult to drive 4-wheel drive Type 53. He also did duty as a test driver on newly completed road car chassis.
As I mentioned, this was a dangerous period in which to be a race driver. How did René deal with it?

After describing in his well written autobiography "My Two Lives" the terrible day at Monza in 1933 when Giuseppe Campari, Baconin Borzacchini and René's friend Count Stanislas Czaykowski were killed in accidents, René went on to say "In racing, the tragedies cannot be long dwelt upon, by its participants at least.
The sport would be finished otherwise. The heart may be heavy, but the world continues".
For 1935 René signed with Scuderia Ferrari to drive the Alfa Romeo P3s, and was married to Gilberte Miraton or, more simply, Chou-Chou.
In his year with Ferrari René collected two victories - Reims and Dieppe - and many top-four finishes which was typical

→

Sport story

of this sensitive driver, who had the ability to take a car to its limits whilst avoiding mechanical problems. The Frenchman was ready to sign for the Scuderia Ferrari for 1936 but political pressures were growing within Europe.

Uncomfortable in Italy, René turned down the second year of the Alfa ride - though he did complete a few drives for Enzo Ferrari - and raced instead for Lago and Talbot, suffering from the cars' unreliability.

In 1937 the Frenchman teamed up with a pair of expatriate Americans living in Paris. Lucy and Laury Schell were the parents of Harry Schell, against whom I raced in the 1950's, and they wanted to create a team that would compete with a new series of Delahayes.

René agreed to be their chief driver which involved him not only in Grand Prix races, but also the Le Mans 24 Hours and the Monte Carlo Rally.

He also signed a deal to race 1500 cc voiturettes for Maserati which he drove to victory in Tripoli and Florence.

With the Delahaye V-12 Grand Prix car René won the famous Million Franc prize at the Pau Grand Prix in 1938. He was also crowned Champion of France.

As hostilities broke out in Europe, René dutifully joined the French army and managed to split military and driving duties. Lucy Schell then convinced the French army to let René go to America to race in the Indianapolis 500.

He sailed to the U.S. on the Conte di Savoia in May, 1940 with another team member who would make a name for himself in America, Luigi Chinetti.

At Indy, confusion over the track's very different rules caused problems, as did a thrown rod in his Maserati during practice, but in the end René was classified 10th that year.

With the German invasion of France, the racing driver decided to stay in the U.S. René opened his first restaurant in America, called the Red Coach Tavern, but soon joined the American army. If you know anything about the military, you will understand that joining the army whilst speaking English, being part of the allies' invasion of Europe and being discharged after the war with the rank of Master Sergeant is no mean feat.

René's sister Suzanne and his brother Maurice emigrated to America. Both joined him in his first New York City

Above, Dreyfus in action with his Bugatti at the Gasometer corner during the 1933 Monaco Grand Prix in which he finished third. In the small photo on the facing page, the French driver, in cap and goggles, waits while the mechanics complete the final checks on his Type 51 before lining up on the starting grid.

restaurant, Le Gourmet. Divorced from Chou-Chou during the war, René married again, this time to Peggy Moros, though she was to die of Hodgkin disease within two years. In 1953 René and Maurice opened their second restaurant, Le Chanteclair, and established once and for all a place for the automotively inclined to dine in New York.

René would be involved with racing on an occasional basis, and even drove at Sebring twice in Arnolt-Bristols, but essentially he was a restaurateur and into the second of what he called "My Two Lives". Incidentally, he was also awarded the French Legion of Honor by Charles de Gaulle during this time for his driving feats during the 1930's.

Back then there were no non-stop flights to Europe, so a stop-over in New York was common for those of us headed that way, and never complete without dinner at Le Chanteclair.

It was usual to meet someone from the automotive world at the restaurant, but my favourite stop there involved a private meeting between René and I.

On my way back from Europe in 1961, I had the King Leopold trophy, which the winner of the Belgian Grand Prix was allowed to keep for a year.

When I got to the restaurant I told René that we must have a drink, but he replied that he wouldn't have a drink until after working hours.

I had a surprise for him, however, and took the trophy out of the bag.

There on the trophy was inscribed my name, alongside those of many of the great drivers of the 1930's, including René. We raised a glass of champagne to the occasion.

Le Chanteclair closed in 1979, and the next year René and Maurice were in Monaco to celebrate the 50th anniversary of his win in that famous race.

Though retired and devoted to his brother, René stayed quite active in automotive events, so we had the chance to talk several times a year, and each meeting was a pleasure.

Now René is gone.

Part of me knows we should be thankful that we had him for so many years, and that he retained his enthusiasm, fine memory and excellent health for all but the last few days of his 88 years. So maybe I'm just being greedy, but I do feel a great sadness at René's passing.

I wish I could telephone him again to ask him about some long past event, some episode about a long-dead racing hero. To hear him recall the past with astonishing clarity, right down to the colors and sounds of the day.

And I'll never forget our last conversation. Having heard he would be having surgery for a coronary aneurysm, I telephoned and said I had heard he was "indisposed". With his typical honesty René pointed out that this would be "...the most difficult race of my life, and Maurice will be there to drop the starting flag". The next day René Dreyfus died during surgery. Remember that it wasn't just a dignified, dapper gentleman who passed away that day, but a giant from the age of the titans.

Art Gallery

LIFE AND MOVEMENT IN THE PASTELS OF FERREYRA-BASSO

In 1990 the painter Jorge Ferreyra-Basso came to the attention of enthusiasts of art and automobiles with a sketch that was chosen as the official poster for the 1000 Miglia retrospective. A realist draughtsman, Ferreyra-Basso succeeded in transforming his boyhood dream into an artistic reality. His works continue to meet with critical success and the admiration of the greats of the automotive world.

BY MARIO MERLO

The true artist, in whatever field he works, can hardly fail to be dominated by the desire to pass on to his contemporaries and those who come after him his own personal message. Independently of any critical judgements, artists tend generally to hand down something of their aesthetic and formative beliefs. The true, thinking artist hopes that his message will be received and passed on as a sign of success and personal achievement.

You could therefore argue that the cultural, figurative and pictorial language of a true artist represents an organized system for the transmission of signs, formulas, tendencies and interpretative symbols in support of the theses that have characterized his activity, as well as his didactic assumptions

It is a fact that artists of any talent whatsoever always attempt to colour reality with the addition of a touch of creative imagination.

It is in the light of these considerations that another foreign artist is introduced to our "Bugatti Art Gallery", Jorge Ferreyra-Basso, an artist with something new to say in the expressive field. Ferreyra-Basso was born at Buenos Aires, Argentina on 20 July, 1943 and currently lives at Bishofsheim in Germany.

He works as head of the drawing office and colour and interiors department at the Opel Styling Centre at Russelheim. His passion for cars is deep rooted and had already emerged during his adolescence in South America. At twenty years of age, whilst studying engineering, the young Jorge drew attention to himself as a brilliant designer, creating competition cars for a number of European teams.

As soon as he graduated he was taken on by the design department of General Motors Argentina, subsequently moving within the same corporation firstly to the Chevrolet division, and then to the German Opel division.

Ferreyra began painting for purely artistic motives in 1975, preferring from the very beginning to deal with classic cars of which he succeeded in rendering the

→

On the facing page, the Bugatti Type 32 Tank from 1923 caught at full speed by the beautiful pastels of Jorge Ferreyra-Basso. The Argentine artist always succeeds in lending his action pictures great vigour.

BUGATTI TYPE 32 "TANK" (1923)

The lively and manoeuvrable Bugatti Type 37 A of 1927, has given and continues to give great satisfaction to those lucky enough to drive it. On the left is Ferreyra's interpretation of this "little" thoroughbred racer.

subtle appeal, often blending the colours in his pictures with his hands.

"Whilst I paint" says Ferreyra-Basso, "I take refuge in another world and since I've been working as a designer in the automotive industry I've found a kind of ideal balance between my own creativity and professional demands in the reinterpretation of these oldtimers.

My hands are my working tools, and the chalks and pastels the ideal instruments with which to express the emotions I feel, almost as if they were the driving force of an engine destined to infuse my paintings with life and movement."

One of the unmistakable characteristics of Jorge Ferreyra-Basso's sporting and automotive painting lies in the fact that the artist often animates the backgrounds of his pictures with portraits of the personalities that conceived, produced or raced the cars depicted.

Here his intent is to pay tribute to their creative genius, their skill or their bravery. Ferreyra-Basso often places the cars in landscape or architectural settings which have the capacity to express a stylistic, historical or emotive link between the machine and its surroundings.

It is a very personal technique which may on occasion be questionable, but one which has certainly brought fame and fortune to the artist. It hardly needs to be

The Argentine painter animates the backgrounds of his pictures with portraits of the personalities directly linked to the car depicted. In this case Ettore Bugatti himself and his son Jean appear in Ferreyra's tribute to the splendid Royale with coupé chauffeur Napoleon coachwork.

LE PÈRE, LE FILS ET LA COUPÉ NAPOLEON

added that his works have been admired not only in the United States, but also in Europe and in Japan, being warmly received by the greats of the automotive world: Enzo Ferrari, Juan Manuel Fangio, Nuccio Bertone, Huschke Von Hainstein, Prince Metternich and others.

It should be noted that Jorge Ferreyra-Basso achieved widespread fame in 1990 thanks to the sketch for a poster which was chosen as the official poster for the 1000 Miglia retrospective.

A year later he produced a successful series of posters on behalf of the organizers of a number of well known historic car events such as the California Mille, the Milas d'Argentina, the American Historic Car Grand Prix and the Monterey Historic Races held at Laguna Seca in California. In 1992 the artist produced among others, the poster for the Wiesbaden International Oldtimers Rally as well as that for Germany's largest and most important historic car event, the Oldtimer Grand Prix.

His works were thus present at the international events richest in tradition and history, making no small contribution to the increasing fame and prestige of the artist among those working in the sector and enthusiasts in general.

Today Ferreyra-Basso prefers working in

→

Art Gallery

Right, the elegant nose of the Type 57; below, the Type 55, and bottom, the Type 44 as seen by Ferreyra-Basso.

pastels on Canson paper, which he defines as "a fascinating and beautiful medium". The paintwork of the cars in his pictures assumes luminous almost silk-like qualities. He has exhibited his works in a number of major German cities - Wiesbaden, Mainz, Aschaffenburg, Eppstein, Essen, Bad, Homburg and others - as well as at the Nürburgring Automobile Museum from October 1985 to October 1986 where his paintings were hung alongside the cars they depicted (from the Bugatti Type 35 B to the Ferrari 250 SWB, from the Maserati 450 S and 300 to the BMW 328 and the Aston Martin DB4).

Ever since the beginning of his painting career (1975), Ferreyra has favoured the sports and competition cars that have made a mark on the technological and stylistic history of the automobile.

As mentioned earlier, his working tools were his fingers and pastels, and his hands immediately began blending tones and colours to create a delicate picture

The collection of Bugatti pastels is completed by the official poster for the Argentine Mille Miglia (left), the Type 57 Coupé Atlantic (below) and the Type 35 in action during the Targa Florio of 1926.

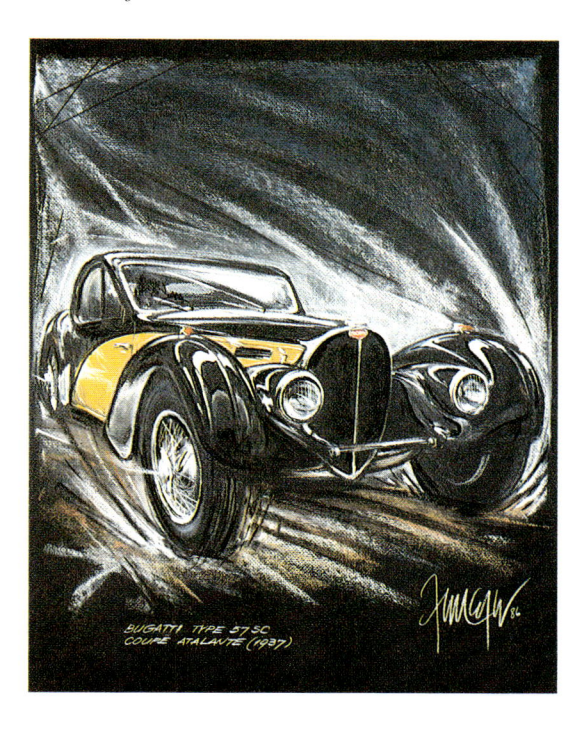

surface which helped him to translate his emotive sensations onto paper.

All the cars he sketched were worked on until they were infused with an original vitality and were, above all, given a sense of location.

In September, 1986, the artist was invited to exhibit his works on the occasion of the opening of the Ettore Bugatti Museum at Molsheim, and the following November at the official opening of the Juan Manuel Fangio Museum in Argentina. Ferreyra-Basso was quickly captivated by the legendary Bugattis, especially at Molsheim, as they represented exemplars of enormous international prestige in the fields of art and transportation technology. In the specific case of the thoroughbreds created by the Molsheim genius, Jorge Ferreyra-Basso, an Argentine artist resident in Germany, a designer and painter of cars, surpassed himself in the creation of images of extraordinary pictorial and evocative power.

Strategy and image

NEW BLUE SENSATIONS

The company's boutique represents an exceptional showcase for the display of the Bugatti treasure. It has been designed in harmony with the company style with blue lacquer and old gold as distinctive traits. The materials selected include lacquered wood, steel and tempered glass. Lighting plays a fundamental role.

BY RENATA ARTIOLI

Above, a view of the Bugatti boutique clearly showing the luminosity of the showroom and the elegance of the furnishings. On the facing page, examples of leather goods and clothing on display.

The Bugatti world is composed of enchanting, precious objects. From the legendary cars to precious metals and the finest leathers, from the captivating colours of soft cloths to pure crystal glass and fine porcelain; the most exclusive range of products ever conceived for the luxury goods sector. A suitable container was required to house and protect this unique treasure; one that would allow its rare qualities to be fully appreciated and discreetly highlighted. It was a stimulating project and the idea that gradually came to dominate the design process influenced the entire conception of the furnishings. A basic symbol was devised, an arc, a frame for these refined works of art and given form and substance in lacquered wood. The symbol was then repeated. It was conjugated according to the spaces

→

to be enclosed and declined in diverse dimensions in proportion to the products, interpreted almost as if was a melody to be played on various instruments. The frame thus became a leitmotif of form and colour - blue and old gold. Light grey was then introduced for the elements completing the furnishings. The designers based their palette on the blue beloved of the Bugatti family, whilst the materials were based around the careful selection of three primary elements: lacquered wood, steel and tempered glass.
The image of the Bugatti Collection boutique was thus fashioned in perfect harmony with the company style. A sober yet sumptuous crown, a module adaptable in terms of dimensions and appearance to any specific space, in any country throughout the world where the Bugatti style is destined to arrive. The atmosphere generated by the finished project is one of agreeable hospitality; the materials such as the smooth, cool lacquer and the soft upholstery fabrics are pleasant to the touch. The forms are sinuous and streamlined and are reflected and repeated in a space rendered infinite by the wall mirrors.
We have created a space in which one immediately gains a sense of refinement and luxurious simplicity.
The compositions enclosed in the frames

The photos on these pages show the forms and colours of the Bugatti furnishings which are in perfect keeping with the exclusive products in the EB Collections.

are richly illuminated by small spotlights as are the interiors of the jewellery cases and the shelves holding the glassware. Thus the lighting has also been carefully studied and plays a major part in the overall composition.
It emphasises forms, softens the angles and lends warmth to the colours.

If we were to define the Bugatti Collection Boutique we could describe it as a treasure chest.
It has been designed according to the same criteria used for all the objects created by our Styling Centre: attention to detail, sobriety and quality of materials.

A TEMPLE FOR THE BUGATTI COLLECTIONS

The Bugatti boutique in the heart of the French capital with its hospitable and sophisticated atmosphere. The great interest aroused by its inauguration.

BY GUALTIERO COPPE

Above, the entrance to the Parisian showroom established by Bugatti in Rue Lamennais: neo-classical style with a hint of empire to underline the Boutique sophisticated elegance. The smaller photos show two views of the classical, functional interior furnishings.

Tympanum, architrave and three columns. A Greek temple? No, it is simply what the French call a "hôtel particulier Directoire" and houses the first showroom dedicated exclusively to the EB Bugatti Collections.
Situated in Rue Lamennais, in the heart of Paris close to l'Etoile, the showroom represents the first important goal in a project involving the creation of a further two exposition centres for the EB Bugatti Collections located in the cosmopolitan cities of Milan and New York. The inauguration was brilliantly organised by Monsieur Jubineau and Madame de la Palme, the directors of the Parisian showroom, and aroused great interest among the international press, the celebrities present and the public.
The building has recently been renovated inside and out. The architecture is neo-classical, tinged with a hint of the empire style. The interior of the showroom is arranged on two levels. There is a spacious and hospitable ground floor illuminated through a glazed frontage, and the mezzanine which is reached via an elegant marble staircase. Warm, diffused lighting and a hospitable and sophisticated atmosphere: a perfect setting for the EB Ettore Bugatti Collections. The EB Ettore Bugatti showroom has a double role to play in serving both operators in the luxury goods sector and the general public passing by in Rue Lammenais in the Paris' 8° arrondissement.

Fashion and Style

A GLOBAL CONCEPTION OF BEAUTY AND FUNCTION

The new Autumn-Winter Collection is a tribute to the art of Carlo Bugatti and features numerous references to the origins of the marque. Prestigious items of clothing and accessories offering high quality materials and exclusive design. Design research transforms tradition into opulence with eloquent colour variations and unusual combinations of the antique and the modern.

BY GIUSEPPE MAGHENZANI

The expressive connotations of a collection can be discussed from various points of view; you can go into materials, fashion trends or use and usage. However, among the myriad symbols submerging our daily lives, each time we seriously set out to make a considered acquisition of a product we are looking for the specific quality of maturity. A product that satisfies on all levels be it tactile, visual, intellectual or intuitive. This needs to be borne in mind if we are to appreciate the difference between the new autumn-winter EB Collections 1994-95, recently presented within the ambit of the Milano Collezioni and the run-of-the-mill market offerings. There are plenty of motives for this kind of reflection: the difficult economic situation, the need to reclaim the most noble of materials in all their great dignity, and the abandonment of a taste often so ephemeral as to penalise judgements of quality. Moreover, in recent years many so-called luxury goods have often survived on their names alone. True quality, the quality that has no need of

→

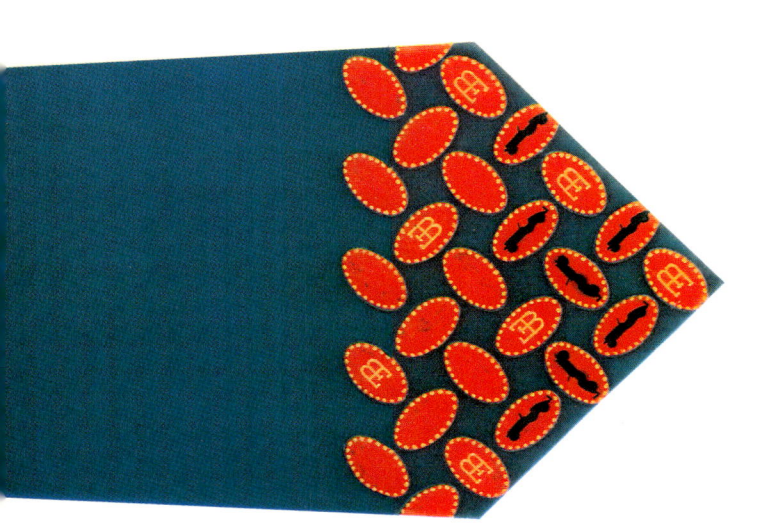

ostentation, has often been obscured by a tidal wave of irrational consumption. The fact is that after years of tendencies, we all feel the need for certainties. This concept is all the more valid when dealing with items of truly high quality clothing, especially when they are created according to a series of values such as the quality of the materials and respect for their aesthetic nature, the practicality and originality of the design and the attention to production details. If alongside these values there exists a profound marque culture then the doors are open to a world of excellence as is the case with the new Ettore Bugatti Collection Uomo. Thus in all of the articles presented art and propriety are combined in an evocation of the Bugatti world.

"Hommage a Carlo Bugatti" offers us a hint of the central theme: the spirit of Carlo is, in fact, present in all the work by Rembrandt, Ettore and Jean. It involves a desire to go back to ones roots the better to affront the new. This reflection on the origins of the legend merits, on the other hand, consideration that goes beyond the importance of the creations typical of Carlo and his age. What is particularly striking in this approach

is the treasure trove of references, inlays, colours and material tones that emerges from the initial contact with the marque's roots. The beauty of the new collection arouses something akin to wonder, forged as it is on the basis of a perfect synthesis of new functional values and "historic" aesthetic elements.
A sense of classicism permits the current stylistic research to comprehend its own tradition and transform it into riches. In the case of the Collection Uomo, this approach is evident, for example, in the interpretation of the finest yarns and wools (cashmere, alpaca and camel-hair), the softest leathers and the warmest and most attractive fabrics. The choice of materials itself plays and important role in the search for functionality: the use of stretch fabrics allowing greater freedom and wearability in the trousers specifically designed for driving is a case in point. The cut of the external pockets, for example, has been reversed to allow the opposite hand to be inserted easily whilst driving. It should be underlined that the Bugatti Styling Centre has deliberately concentrated its efforts on a restricted and highly

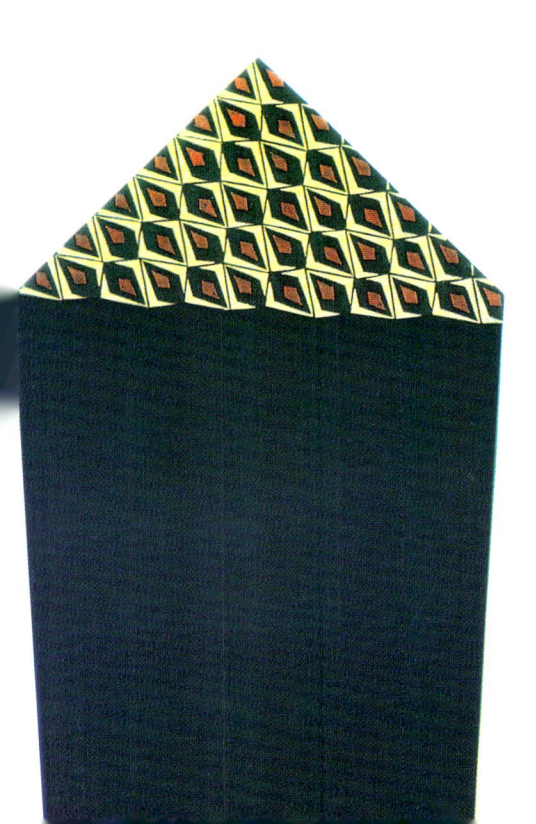

→

specific range of basic clothing. This theme has been explored by the Bugatti team and the production heads of the partner companies, together with the Collection's Art Director Nicola Grillo. This allowed distribution questions to be answered at the design stage. The Collection boasts excellent knitwear and a careful selection of leather articles, and is thus not simply a study of fashion trends but a complex entrepreneurial undertaking; "Hommage a Carlo Bugatti" is a global conception of the Bugatti image. We are referring, for example, to the work of Frau with the suitcases and Mantero with the ties: both firms have contributed to and shared in the success of the Ettore Bugatti Collection Uomo. Two features are particularly worthy of note: the functional transformability of many of the articles and the "transformability" of the spirit of Carlo in the textures of the knitwear and the tie Collection. Painstaking research into construction techniques offered the possibility of revolutionizing the potential of jackets or waistcoats which can be magically transformed into rucksack-containers; the ties and scarves, on the other hand, are the backdrop for a virtuoso display of the spirit of Carlo. The initial

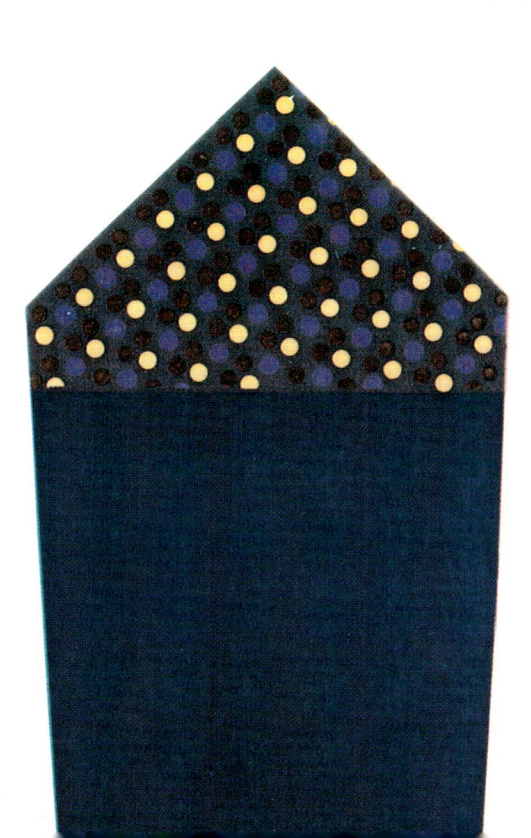

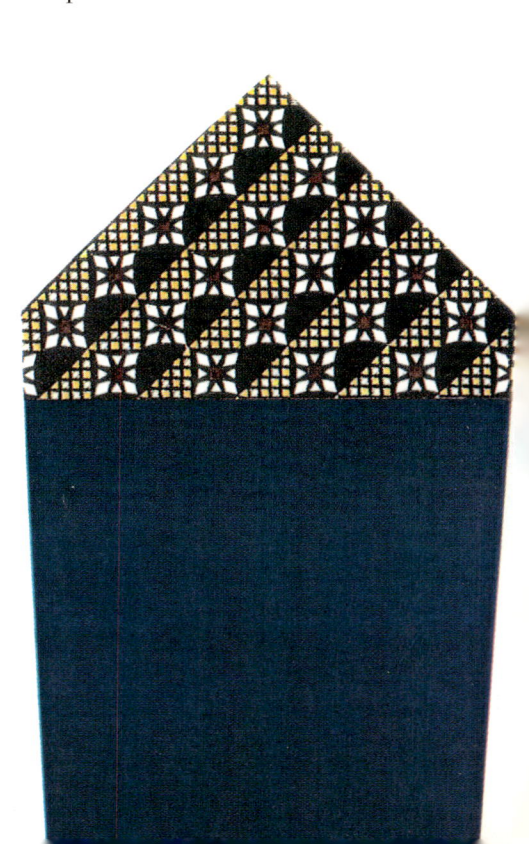

textures are born out of two archetypes dear to Ettore's father: the wings of the dragonfly and certain geometrical figures. Their development has led to the creation of an enchanting range of ties (15 printed motifs and 36 in Jacquard weaves).
As you can see in the photos, the motifs derived from Carlo Bugatti have been flanked by others deriving from the automotive traditions and the iconography of the marque itself (the "EB" monogram, the Red Oval and the radiator). Naturally, the same high standards of manufacture and care in the selection of premium quality materials applies to the ties.
The creative process behind them took into account not only the perfection of the design, but also the most suitable support for the motif. Thus an extremely fine Jacquard weave was chosen to support an equally finely drawn design, whilst in coordinating every detail with the marque, an EB texture was incorporated into the ties' internal support. Checks, backgrounds and combinations of ancient and modern, have all been carefully chosen to lend the Collection an exclusive elegance in keeping with the Bugatti tone and spirit.

New agreements

MANTERO AND THE BUGATTI SILK ROAD

*On the basis of a recent creative and commercial deal, all Bugatti's silk products will be manufactured by Mantero of Como, a leading company in the silk sector.
The elegant new collections of scarves and ties recently presented at Milan are already enjoying gratifying international success.*

BY ROBERTO MERLO

When Ettore competed with his cars in the early years of the century he would wear a silk scarf to protect his face from the wind and dust. This was no mere whim but a positive statement of style and functionality that was so often a feature of the Molsheim genius' career and lifetime. The idea developed by the Ora Styling Centre was that of offering today's Bugatti enthusiasts a particular quality of silk that would be light, crease-proof and hard wearing, with splendid colours and designs, as well as pleasant to the touch and classically elegant.

The powers that be at Bugatti could hardly have chosen a better partner for this ambitious project than Mantero of Como, a large, modern company with a family tradition stretching back nearly 100 years. A company producing the world's most beautiful and prestigious silks. Over three generations the Mantero

Below, set in a brightly coloured symphony of Mantero silk, a historic image of Ettore Bugatti the driver with a classic silk scarf used to protect his face during competition.

family has succeeded in developing, with unmatched skill and craftsmanship, the demanding and sophisticated art of silk weaving, bringing it to a peak of technical expression and creativity.

"Operating in a highly competitive and continuously developing market such as textiles", comments Riccardo Mantero, the eldest of 5 brothers and the President of the group, "it is of the utmost importance to maintain, plan and guarantee the highest levels of quality. We believe that quality is not something that applies to just the final product, but is rather an intrinsic aspect of the business culture that permeates throughout the company's activities."

Mantero is today the world leader in the production and marketing of high quality →

silk fabrics.
The group has a turnover of 338 billion lire, employs 1,135 people and exports 57% of its total production. The Como-based firm boasts a strong vertically-organized structure with no less that 4 factories.
The strength of the Mantero-Bugatti agreement lies in the relationship established between Ora and Como. The creative staff of the two companies who have worked side-by-side on the creation of the new collections, immediately enjoyed a perfect understanding.

EB

According to Cesare Alessandroni, the Como firm's Marketing Director, "Mantero's vertical integration process is one of the principal guarantees of absolute product quality that Bugatti has recognized in our firm.

Mantero is capable of overseeing all the complex silk production processes, from the examination of the raw materials to the spinning of the yarns, from the weaving to the dyeing, from the printing to the finishing.
Furthermore we have been able to offer Bugatti the help of a team of skilled specialists capable, on the basis of the input from the Ora Styling Centre, of correctly interpreting the Bugatti world and translating and integrating it into fabric products such as ties and scarves."
Bugatti wants to avoid becoming a designer label as it holds to a completely different philosophy: that of creating and marketing an elegant, functional collection that will endure over time,

Top, the printing of the silk scarves in the Mantero factory at Grandate. In this delicate phase of the operation each colour is applied individually to obtain perfect colouration and accuracy in the final product. In the small photo, one of the classic scarves from the Mantero Collection.

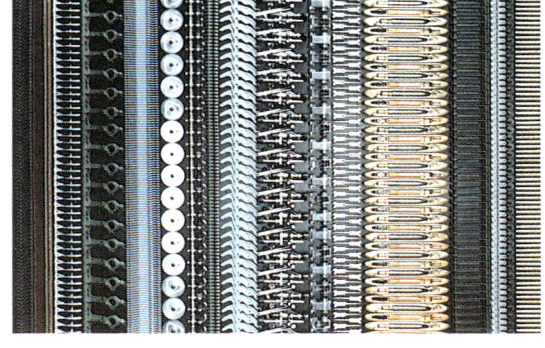

In the small photos on this page; top, some of the scarves produced by Mantero using the most sophisticated technology; centre, a selection of fabrics for ties; below, the characteristic panel-sculpture produced by ingegnere Federico Mantero using sections of screen frames.

thereby propagating and confirming, through a distinct personality, the immortal style and culture of the Bugatti era. The ties and scarves represent ideal means of expressing and promoting the character and image of the Bugatti universe through suitable graphic designs.

We are not therefore dealing with one of any number of fashion labels, but rather a prestigious marque with an impeccable image, tradition and culture destined to occupy a rarefied market sector.

The Ettore Bugatti team has concentrated, as was only to be expected, on exclusive, high class, elegant, refined and sophisticated products.

The agreement with Mantero is therefore the logical consequence of a well defined policy. The Como company, with its centenarian tradition of artistic talent and craftsmanship, with its constant, painstaking attention to detail and its highly developed concept of quality has, from Bugatti's point of view, represented an ideal point of reference for the development of classic style with a notable artistic heritage.

The essence of the Bugatti-Mantero agreement can be found here.

Meetings and events

BUGATTI: A MARRIAGE OF STYLE AND CULTURE

The Bugatti legend continues to expand. The EB Donna and Uomo Collections make their debuts in Milan, the spiritual home of designer fashion. The Istituto Europeo di Design holds the successful Bugatti & Bugatti exhibition. Powerful amplifiers reproduced the roar of the Bugatti engines at the Bolzano Museum on the occasion of "Sound: Forme e Colori del Suono".

BY KARIN SCANZONI

Top, the entrance to the Milano Collezioni, a key event for the fashion world held in September for women's fashions, and in January for menswear, where Bugatti officially presented its new collections.
Right, the unmistakable symbol of the Bugatti radiator makes an unusual frame for the elegant parade of women's wear and accessories.

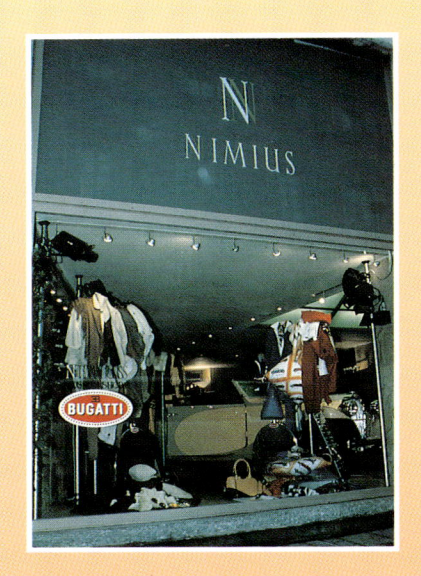

Left, the window of the Nimius Museum Shop in Milan's Via Durini, close to Piazza San Babila. The shop dedicated its entire display to Bugatti products, with the extraordinary presence of the legendary Type 57, the exclusive prize in the Bugatti-Diana De Silva competition. Below, Nimius again, with our magazine together with a model of the Type 50 and a selection of clothing accessories in the foreground.

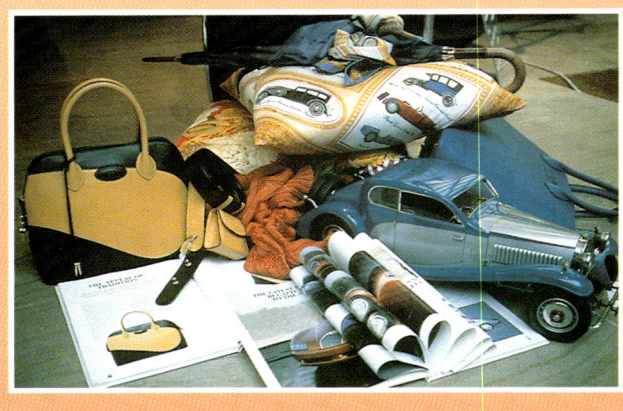

I like the idea that Bugatti has finally emerged from the forgotten depths of the past to enter into the consciousness of even the less attentive, and that when asked the name of the company's founder most people will come up with Ettore spontaneously and without hesitation. But what I find really marvellous is that Bugatti is now a living, evolving legend. The number of people who not only know who Ettore was but can talk knowledgeably of Carlo, Rembrandt and Jean, and therefore of inlays, sculptures, forms and the Bugatti style, is growing daily. It's extraordinary; you get the impression that you are taking part in, perhaps even contributing to, a collective cultural enrichment. The catalyst behind this expansion of awareness of the Bugatti marque has been in part what we have come to call the "Bugatti Events". Ventures that stimulate interest, curiosity and passion in the fields of culture and fashion, thanks in no small part to the creation of the EB Collections in Italy and abroad.

In the photo above, the elegant Franco Maria Ricci bookshop in Milan which housed a Bugatti showroom on the occasion of the Milano Collezioni Donna. Right, personality and style in the Bugatti clothes.

Below, a shot of the exhibition of new Bugatti clothing presented at Milano Collezioni in January.

The EB Collection Donna made its fashion world debut on the occasion of the Milano Collezioni, an event bringing together under one roof all the greatest stylists from around the world. Bugatti was presented to the women's fashion market as a marque rich in history and tradition which, whilst firmly rooted in the past, offers new designs that are at once original, practical and functional. The whole show was tinged with blue thanks to the presence of classic Bugattis and the EB 110, and also met with the approval of the experts in the field. The weeks following the launch of the EB Collection Donna saw two notable events enliven Via Durini in the very heart of Milan's city centre, with the Bugatti products "invading" the F.M.R. shop, considered as Milan publishing's holy of holies. It was impossible not to come across Bugatti displays and replica radiators in the shop windows. There was even the legendary Type 57, the fabulous prize in the Bugatti-Diana De Silva competition, on display at the Nimius Museum shop. Naturally the Bugatti sales outlets in other Italian cities and around the world also offer their clients and all those interested the chance to admire the world's fastest car. These are enthusiastically received ventures held on the occasion of the inauguration of Bugatti sales points, and thus mark the further extension of the retail network.

On this subject specific mention really has to be made of the inauguration of the Bugatti showroom in Paris, situated in the very heart of the French capital, and the appointment of the sole distributor of Bugatti and EB accessories for the Principality of Monaco

The cultural initiatives began with the "Bugatti & Bugatti" exhibition, a historical review which, via references to the form and style which made the marque famous, came up to date with a display of the most recent Bugatti products. The Istituto Europeo di Design opened the doors of its Design Gallery on 15 September, 1993, a significant date for all Bugatti events (it was of course Ettore's birthday).

At the same time the Bolzano Museum was presenting "Sound: Forme & Colori del Suono". In the amphitheatre in front of the museum stood an example of the fantastic EB 110, finished in Bugatti blue of course, whilst powerful amplifiers reproduced the impressive roar of its engine.

Evocative images that met with such success that the Niccoli Art Gallery decided to present the exhibition to the citizens of Parma.

Photo: Maria Cristina Vimercati
Design: Enrico Kkienn Ciceri

VIII MANTERO

COMO

Foulards da collezione